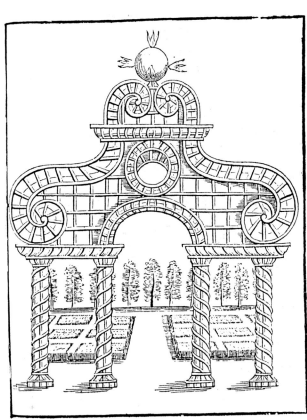

Pergolas, Arbours and Arches

Pergolas, Arbours and Arches

THEIR HISTORY AND HOW TO MAKE THEM

PAUL EDWARDS

KATHERINE SWIFT

with

LINDA FARRAR

SYLVIA LANDSBERG

JAN WOUDSTRA

ROBIN WHALLEY

ANDREW CLAYDEN

with special photography by

JESSICA SMITH

BARN ELMS

Published in 2001 by Barn Elms Publishing
93 Castelnau, London SW13 9EL

Designed by Jessica Smith

Printed in Hong Kong by Midas Printing Ltd

A CIP record of this book is available from the
British Library

ISBN 1 899531 06 8

Endpapers. Illustrations from Jan van der Groen, *Den
Nederlandtsen Hovenier,* first published in 1669.

Title-page. Rose 'Sanders White' immaculately trained
across the pergola at West Dean.

Contents

INTRODUCTION
7
Katherine Swift

KATHERINE SWIFT

Introduction

Annihilating all that's made
To a green Thought in a green Shade

Andrew Marvell (1621-78)

Pergolas, arbours and arches are a source of some of the most acute of all garden pleasures – the visual contrast of architectural line with twining plant, the gardenly satisfactions of plants trimly tied and trained (or wantonly trailing), the sensuous dangling of fruit or flower just within reach – but above all perhaps, of the subtle interweaving of interior and exterior, the special feeling afforded only by structures like these of being both inside and outside at the same time. The experience of walking, sitting or dining beneath such open plant-covered structures is qualitatively different both from the experience of sitting beneath or among trees, and also from the sensation of being within more solid structures or buildings. Inside a pergola or an arbour we are not removed from the sights and sounds and smells of the garden outside, the playful movement of light and shade, the touch of the breeze, the passage of the clouds overhead – indeed we experience all these things with a sort of heightened consciousness, as if the framing device of the structure called our attention to what before was mere vacant air.

Yet always there is that delicious sense of enclosure. These structures invite our participation in the garden: they beckon us to enter, to stroll, to sit, above all to linger. Time slows to a languorous drawl in structures like these. Sitting in a garden without some feeling of enclosure about one is somehow unsettling and unsatisfactory, like sitting in a room without an open fire: we never stay long, never quite settle down to the book or the unwritten page, which glares whitely at us in the plain light of day. Similarly, there is never quite the same feeling of intimacy and ease in a stroll *à deux* out in the open as there is down the long vista of the pergola. And to dine without benefit of the dappled shade provided by pergola or arbour feels somehow perfunctory and spartan, however glorious the weather.

The appeal of such structures is universal and timeless, spanning continents and millennia. And almost from their beginnings in ancient times their frank appeal to our sensuality has been well to the fore. Some of the earliest representations of structures such as these are used to frame scenes of eating and drinking: Greeks and Romans sprawl on their dining couches, the Abyssinian King Ashurbanipal feasts with his queen beneath an arbour of vines, waterside revellers in the Alexandrian resort of Canopus loll beneath ripe grapes and perfumed roses. In the third century AD the Roman writer Achilles Tatius commented on the effects of light and dappled shade, the delicious interplay of coolness and warmth on the skin – an effect carefully stage-managed by Gertrude Jekyll sixteen centuries later. And for centuries their decorative appeal has attracted artists as well as

King Ashurbanipal and his queen feasting under vines in their garden at Nineveh. The stone relief was carved in about 645 BC and seems timeless – though today we might not hang the severed head of an enemy as ornament to such a scene.

gardeners, exploiting the piquant contrast between architectural elements and the soft twining counterpoint of the plants in art works and artefacts from Greek urns to Pre-Raphaelite fabrics and wallpapers.

In medieval Christendom, arbours of all sorts gained an added spiritual dimension as a setting for representations of the Madonna and Child, both bringing the holy figures into the real world in an everyday setting, and in turn enriching the everyday world with the consciousness of the glories of God's creation. In the symbolism of paintings such as Cranach's *Madonna in the vine arbour*, viewers were invited to see the partnership of God and man, paralleled by the partnership of architecture and plant, gardener and nature.

A constant theme is the combination of beauty and utility. With their origins in the ancient cultivation of grapes, such structures were soon adapted as supports for a variety of other climbing plants. Vines and roses were a common combination from ancient times, and many a modern structure has reclaimed for us the decorative possibilities of fruits and climbing vegetables as well as flowers. But beyond their merely horticultural role, pergola-like structures in particular have always fulfilled an important circulatory function in linking (or sometimes separating) the different parts of a site, whether medieval European monastery or castle with its covered

Swags of grapes and ivy surround the al fresco diners on this Greek wine bowl of about 350 BC.

Previous page. Rose 'Blairi No. 2' frames an opening in the pear tunnel in Katherine Swift's garden at the Dower House, Morville.

walks linking different buildings, Chinese garden with its elaborate open-sided *lang*, or twentieth-century western compartmentalised garden with its pergola or arch pointing the way from one garden 'room' to another.

Some of those structures are closer to solid garden buildings, where we find an interior unvaryingly the same within a structure built to last: damp-proofed, roofed over, sometimes walled in. But the pergolas, arbours and arches which are the subject of this book all convey powerful feelings of transitoriness, movement, a sense of the fleeting moment. In certain cultures the plants may be chosen to heighten that sense of transience, as in the traditional Japanese use of wisteria with its fragile fleeting blossoms so transparently at the mercy of frost and rain, tossed by every gust of wind. Elsewhere plants have been chosen in an attempt to deny that essential fact, as in the seventeenth-century European

fashion for tunnels and arbours made from clipped hornbeam – the plant becoming the architecture while the architecture, in the form of ever more fanciful trelliswork, stood alone as an ornament in itself. In contemporary western usage designers have continued to play with ideas of time by making pergolas and arbours on the one hand from dynamic, sustainable structures of living wood such as willow, and on the other from materials such as stainless steel, left un-planted. Open plant-covered structures in contrast respond to the time and the season like the garden itself, the plants burgeoning into leaf, flower and fruit before fading away or lapsing back into winter sleep, the structures themselves gently decaying – iron rusting, wood rotting (whether hazel poles with a life of a year or the most elaborate sawn timber with a life measured in decades), even the most robust of marble pillars at the mercy of toppling winds. They are in themselves little essays in mutability.

A simple fork-pole structure to support vines as seen in an Egyptian tomb found near the pyramids. The medieval fork-pole arbour was the natural successor to these first utilitarian structures.

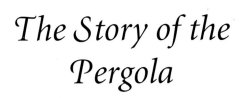

The Story of the Pergola

The two pergolas which flank the Lower Rose Terrace at Bodnant mark the transition from the formal Italianate terraced gardens to the richly luxuriant woodland planting which surrounds them.

LINDA FARRAR

The Pergola in Ancient Rome

I hurried back to the girl. She was in a formal garden adjoining the house. It was in fact a grove of very pleasant aspect, encloistered by a sufficiently high wall and a chorus line of columns that together formed a covered portico on all four sides of the garden. Protected within the columns stood a populous assembly of trees…[fruit trees and a plane tree are mentioned]. *Grapes grew on trellises on either side of the tree, thick-leaved, ripe with fruit whose clusters tumbled through the trelliswork like locks of curly hair. When the highest, sunlit leaves fluttered in the wind, the earth took on a dappled look, with yellow patches in the shade.*

(Achilles Tatius, *Leucippe and Clitophon*, 1, 15)

This extract from a delightful Alexandrian tale of the third century AD has a timeless quality that belies its antiquity. The scene unfolds in the setting of a decorative garden and although the translator of the ancient text has chosen the word 'trellis' it could also be interpreted as a pergola. Evidence from archaeology and ancient literature suggests that these structures could have been found in small and large domestic gardens as well as in public parks throughout the Roman world.

We are fortunate that so much literature has survived of the Roman period and although references to gardens are on the whole tantalisingly short, they can still give a valuable insight into the role of pergolas at that time. The most helpful texts are from Pliny the Elder and Younger (uncle and nephew) and Columella, who wrote a comprehensive manual on agriculture and horticulture. Columella, who was originally a farmer from Gades (modern Cadiz in Spain), gave useful advice for vines grown on pergolas: 'And if there are any *pergulae* of good vines or any single trees mated to vines in the field or thickets left out by the pruners, they should certainly be pruned before April 1st'. (Columella, *On Agriculture*, XI, 2, 32)

As can be seen the Latin word for a pergola was *pergula* (pl. *pergulae*). This word is thought to have come from the verb *pergere*, which means to proceed or go forward, and it is possible that the pergola was originally a lightly built wooden projection from the side of a house. We can see such a structure in an architectural scene in one of the frescoes in the House of the Vettii at Pompeii; in this instance it has been used to support red roses that are shown peeping through the crossed beams. Many Latin words had several meanings, and in the Graeco-Roman period the word *pergula* was used when referring to a flimsy or rickety shelter or cabin made of reeds or sticks in the countryside. As these were regarded as being rather ramshackle, poets would make fun of people born in these lowly abodes. The framework of a pergola could have derived from these humble structures but they soon evolved into a highly decorative art form.

Pergolas, arbours and arches can be dated back to 80 BC at least, when they appear in a mosaic found at Palestrina near Rome (opposite). This large mosaic is thought to have been made by craftsmen from Alexandria, who depicted a Graeco-Roman view of life along the whole course of the river Nile. Towards the end of its course the river reaches the notoriously affluent district of Canopus, and in the mosaic this scene is represented by revellers feasting and drinking under the shade of a beautiful arched trelliswork pergola made of tall reeds covered with vines and roses. Roses were highly prized in antiquity mainly because of their scent and colour, and so it is no surprise to find that they were used in this way to scent the air for those dining al fresco.

The Romans liked to entertain their guests in the garden under a pergola or arbour, especially in hot summer weather, when the cooling shade and fresh air would be greatly appreciated. This is

Couples dining under a vine and rose covered pergola beside the Canopic canal of the Nile in Graeco-Roman Egypt. Detail from the large mosaic found at Palestrina near Rome and dated to around 80 BC. The structure is strikingly similar to Buro Hoppold's 'gridshell' at the Earth Centre (see page 68).

13

clearly shown in a long letter written by Pliny the Younger inviting his friend to come to stay at his villa at Tusculum in Italy. He reveals how proud he was of his gardens and the facilities he had included in their design. In one area, which he named his 'hippodrome' or racecourse (his design mimicked its shape), he had created a wonderful garden with numerous walks, fountains and a special dining area: 'At the upper end of the course is a curved dining couch of white marble, shaded by a vine trained over four slender pillars of Carystian marble'. (Pliny the Younger, *Letters*, V, 6, 36)

This pergola with its marble pillars was special. Most would have been made of wood, but archaeologists have found evidence for both not just at Pompeii (which had been covered by the deep volcanic fallout of AD 79), but also at less well-preserved sites throughout the Roman Empire. At Vienne in France two citizens each decided to furnish their peristyle garden with a summer *triclinium*, a permanent masonry three-sided couch that could accommodate nine people. The diners on both U-shaped couches were protected from the glare of the sun by a large wooden pergola above; presumably this would have had vines or roses climbing over its framework. As in Pliny's outdoor dining area, a fountain playing nearby completed this pleasant setting. A copy of a summer *triclinium* has been created in the palace gardens at Fishbourne in southern Britain. Such rest and recreation areas within a garden were very popular. They could be seen to mimic the shade-giving boughs of a tree (the Latin word for which is *arbor*).

Many Romans enjoyed a luxurious lifestyle, and one of the pleasures of home was to spend time in the garden or its surrounding porticoes. Roman town houses were essentially inward facing so that the garden would act as a source of light for all the rooms around it. The garden in the centre was usually decorative because it would give an attractive view from important reception rooms. Of course if the garden was a large one then there would be greater scope for embellishment. Romans enlivened their gardens in many ways and some of the surviving fresco paintings show how decorative they could be. In a large fresco from Boscoreale, near Pompeii in Italy, there is a marble or stone pergola with an arched top from which

A nineteenth-century reconstruction of the al fresco dining area in the small garden at the House of Sallust, Pompeii.

Below. Oscilla hanging from branches in a small enclosure garden. This drawing is from a miniature fresco in the House of the Golden Cupids in Pompeii.

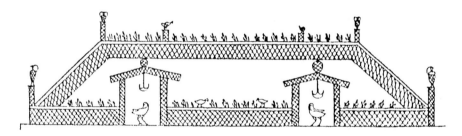

numerous bunches of luscious black grapes are hanging ready to pick (page 17).

There are also several miniature frescoes showing garden enclosures or 'garden rooms' which allow a glimpse of how a garden space was used and how it would have appeared in antiquity. They show how the Romans used decorative trellis fences to create recesses or niches which form ideal places for a bench or to display statuary or an urn. Arbours are created within these gardens and decorative arches and pergolas give access to further sections of the garden. Deliberate eye-catchers were included to form a focal point, or just to decorate the scene, and another idea was to include one or two small carved objects (*oscilla*) which could be hung from an arch, where, as their name suggests, they could oscillate with the breeze and would catch the eye. Painted *oscilla* are seen in miniature garden enclosure scenes found in the House of the Golden Cupids and the House of the Citharist in Pompeii. Interestingly archaeologists

Right. Decorative arches and pergolas separate a series of small garden rooms or enclosures providing spaces to display statuary, urns and topiary. The drawing is taken from a miniature fresco at Pompeii.

Bottom right. A drawing of a miniature fresco from the Auditorium of Maecenas in Rome. The original is now very faded but trellis fences and pergolas surround a rectangular fountain pool.

Right. Photograph of a
miniature fresco from
Herculaneum showing
decorative trellis fences
and pergolas. The drawing
immediately below
shows the whole fresco.

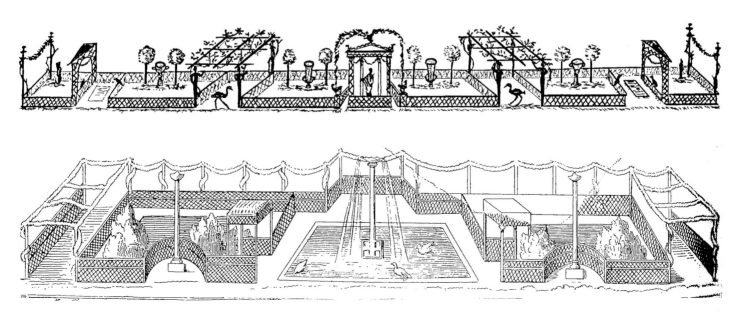

have found that these houses also had a series of real *oscilla* hanging between the columns of their garden porticoes. Time and again archaeological evidence has been found to confirm some feature of the pictures seen in ancient frescoes.

Frescoes show that the most popular plants grown in and around these trellis arbours were laurels (our sweet bay, *Laurus nobilis*); and the rose (*Rosa gallica*, which is known to be ancient). They used sculptural plants such as acanthus and Hart-stongue ferns, together with specimen trees and topiary to accentuate the scene, and as they liked scented plants you would also find aromatic myrtle bushes, white lilies, sweet marjoram, violets and '*hesperis*' (our dame's violet). The Romans searched for new flowering and fruiting plants to acclimatise at Rome, and this early dissemination of plant species is one of their enduring legacies.

The Romans made use of other climbing plants on their trellises and pergolas, such as ivy, which could also be used to climb up poles or trees so that it could be formed into swags. House and garden were decorated on feast days and birthdays and the plentiful supply of ivy, which grows so rapidly, often formed the base to which seasonal flowers could be added. Another climber used to shade a pergola was the gourd. We usually think of this only as a vegetable, but it was also seen as decorative. There are a couple of wonderful catacomb fresco paintings that show the Early Christian scene of Jonah and the gourd tree. In these Jonah is always depicted reclining under a simply made pergola with large gourds hanging above. Although these date to the third-fourth century AD gourds and cucumbers were grown on pergolas much earlier and are mentioned by Pliny the Elder in his mammoth encyclopaedic work on

Jonah reclining under a pergola supporting gourds. The semicircular frame is composed of three rose garlands tied with a knot. This fresco dates from the fourth century AD and is from the Via Latina Catacomb in Rome.

Right. These decorative gourds, photographed at Helmingham Hall in Suffolk follow a long tradition. The gourds of the Roman period originated in Africa and would have been *Lagenaria siceraria*.

Far right. An elaborate square columned vine-covered pergola with luscious black grapes. It is a key feature in this garden fresco originally painted in the first century BC on a bedroom wall in a villa at Boscoreale.

A pergola shading an elongated fish pool and al fresco dining area to the rear on the upper terrace at the House of Loreius Tiburtinus in Pompeii.

Reconstructed pergolas at either side of a series of inter-communicating pools in the lower garden at the House of Loreius Tiburtinus in Pompeii.

natural history in the first century AD. Pliny says: 'They have not the strength to stand without supports, but they shoot up at a rapid pace, covering bowers and pergolas wih a light shade'. (Pliny the Elder, *Natural History*, XIX, 24, 69)

The Romans liked both decorative and utilitarian qualities, so gourds and cucumbers would not necessarily have been confined to the humble vegetable garden. Also the grapes grown on pergolas in gardens could be harvested to make wine. Pliny the Elder provides a noteworthy example that relates to a portico garden that had been donated to the public by the Empress Livia, wife of Augustus: 'And a thing that was considered in the first degree worthy of record… is that a single vine in the Portico of Livia at Rome protects the open walks with its shady pergolas, while at the same time it produces twelve amphorae of juice yearly'. (Pliny the Elder, *Natural History*, XIV, 3, 11). Public parks were much frequented by all of society and this extract shows that they could be functional as well as ornamental. Tavern keepers in both town and country also found they could increase custom by providing a shady al fresco area for refreshments. Virgil immortalises such a scene where the innkeeper tempts passing customers to his premises: 'There are garden nooks and arbours, mixing-cups, roses, flutes, lyres and cool bowers with shady reeds…. Come ; rest here thy wearied frame beneath the shade of vines'. (Virgil, *Copa*, 7-8 and 29)

Pergolas, arbours and arches remained popular right through the long period of the Roman Empire, and a chance find at Cyrene in Libya (then a province of Rome) reveals that they continued in favour into the fifth century AD. Here Hesychius, a prominent citizen of the town, had created a wonderful paradise garden set in the very heart of his home. At one side of his peristyle garden he had built a permanent curved dining couch and fountain pool protected from the fierce southern sun by a shady pergola. This was approached by a short paved pathway, which was also protected and decorated by a pergola supported by four pairs of marble columns. He must have been proud of these arrangements for the pergolas occupied at least one third of the garden space. They would have made quite an impact on his dining guests.

Unfortunately this garden is a bit ruinous today, but at Pompeii the pergolas in the House of Loreius Tiburtinus have been reconstructed (from archaeological evidence found there) so we are able to visualise their appearance and see how effective they were. The garden here consists of two terraces, on the upper terrace a vine-covered pergola protects an elongated pool and outdoor dining area. At about midway there is a little shrine, below which is a fountain. Steps near here lead down to the lower terrace with a continuous pergola on either side of a long series of interconnecting pools stretching to the full length of the garden. Irises have been planted alongside the pools, and the whole is very effective. It is truly a beautiful sight.

Gregory of Nysa, writing in the fourth century AD, was clearly impressed when he saw a similar sight at Vantona (in modern Turkey). He imitates Pliny the Younger with a lengthy description of the estate he visits:

Who could find words worthy to describe the path under the climbing vines, and the sweet shade of their cluster, and that novel wall structure where roses with their shoots, and vines with their trailers, twist themselves together…and the pond at the summit of this path, and the fish that are bred there?

(Gregory of Nysa, *Nicene and Post-Nicene Fathers of the Christian Church*, Letter XV)

SYLVIA LANDSBERG

Medieval Pergolas, Arbours and Arches

Left. Lucas Cranach: *Madonna in the vine arbour, c.1500.* The Madonna is shown in a seat arch formed from curved laths which support vines. The upright laths are tied at the top, and to cross laths, with withies. The seat front shows other typical construction materials – stout poles and carpenter's work planks.

Right. St Elizabeth with her son John the Baptist in a coppice-pole arbour of roses. This is a full-page miniature added in a Book of Hours from the workshop of Jean Colombe at Bourges, late fifteenth century.

Although covered walks were an important feature in medieval gardens the word 'pergola' was not itself in use, while 'arbour' had a wider meaning than it does now and was used to describe either a canopied seating area or a covered garden walk or even the whole enclosed garden.

Our information on medieval gardens is scanty and fragmentary, but it has been possible to develop a body of knowledge by correlating texts that are for the most part English with illustrations that are almost all continental. To this we can add the insight gained from watching those present-day rural craftsmen who still work with medieval materials and who are employing medieval practices handed down over the generations but never written down.

Medieval documents about building work occasionally mention the purchase of timber and poles, whether for supports for vines, or for 'coumbles' (roofs) or 'le crouches' for vines (probably trellis tunnels), or for materials for the making and mending of 'alleys' (walks) covered with vines. The vocabulary depends on the particular clerk who is recording the details. A thumbnail sketch by the Flemish chronicler Froissart on visiting Eltham Palace in 1395 brings such brief notes to life when he describes walking up and down in the garden 'where it was very pleasant and shady, for those alleys were then covered in vines'.

The earliest guidance on the positioning of shady walks within gardens comes from Albertus Magnus, a much travelled abbot, re-expositing in about 1260 an earlier incomplete work written by the encyclopaedist Bartholomew the Englishman in 1240. Here it is stated that trees should be planted and vines trained round the edge of the lawn to give 'a delightful cooling shade', leaving 'lightness and airiness' in the centre.

The written Albertus ideal of peripheral walks is backed up visually by our earliest garden plan, a monastic one, of Christ Church Priory, Canterbury, in 1165 – a century earlier (page 22). It seems feasible that the traditional monastic cloister design could have given birth to the secular idea of peripheral shade trees and vine-shaded walks. In fact architectural cloister walks were also

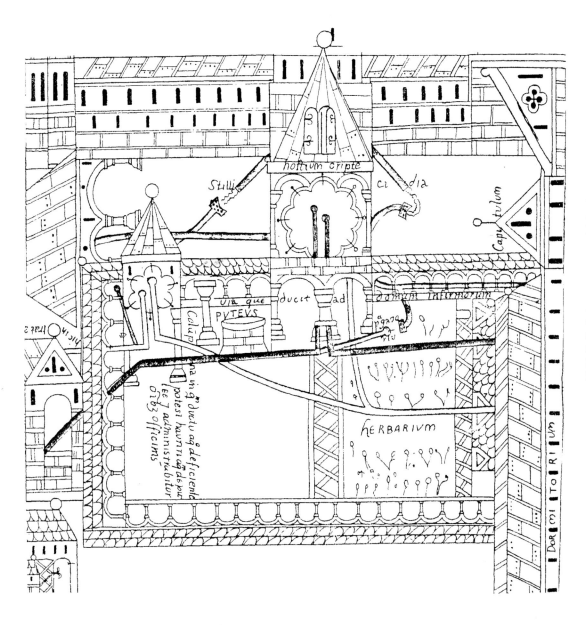

Left. Part of Wibert's plan of 1165 of the waterworks at Christ Church Priory, Canterbury. Here the archetypal two-part garden of the infirmary is composed of a lawn and a herb garden. Shady cloister walks and a free-standing stone and tile pergola form the perimeter. A central trellis pergola allows a complete stroll round each half of the garden.

Right above. The flat top of the timber-framed tunnel arbour at Tretower Court supports a mature canopy of *Rosa* x *alba*. Diagonal oak-lath trellises line the walks.

Right below. Detail from *St John baptising the infants* by Lorenzo and Jacomo Salimbeni. An open-sided pole arbour with forked uprights supports a ceiling of vines. To the left a light-weight cane arbour with a flat roof similarly shades the drinkers.

to be found in royal gardens, for instance marble ones in the fourteenth-century manor of Guildford, and again at Sheen Palace.

In the Christ Church plan there is also a free-standing walk of some architectural quality and a subdividing trellised strip, likely to indicate a pergola walk in that it completes two shady paths: one round the lawn and the other round the herb garden. This interpretation helps to clarify the types of covered walk found in medieval gardens.

The first type resulted from the nature of monastic, palace and castle buildings, where different domestic functions were housed in separate buildings. For convenience these were connected by covered ways which were normally built attached to walls, as for instance between the kitchens and the Great Hall of Clarendon Palace. These 'lean-to' structures were called cloisters, pentices (*appenticium*) or galleries. They were framed of timber or stone and roofed with lead or, alternatively, clay, oak or stone tiles or even timber weatherboarding.

The second type provided support for plants which merely shaded the walks rather than

making them weatherproof. For royalty or nobility such pergolas could be of 'carpenter's work', that is, jointed timber, which was extravagant both in materials and labour. But the most common type, even amongst the wealthy, were arched tunnel pergolas of basket-like appearance, made from curved coppice poles of sufficient strength to support vines and roses (pages 24, 29 and 31). These tunnels were usually free-standing, but are occasionally illustrated attached to walls.

Pergolas are for walking through, but the word 'arbour', as we know it, usually implies a canopied seating area. Whilst single benches, sometimes with a cantilevered overhead canopy, are occasionally illustrated in medieval times, the more usual form of seating was built round three sides of a square. A loggia was the name given when such seats were incorporated, roofed, as part of a building. Kiosks or summerhouses were free-standing three-sided sitting places of timber or stone – sometimes even with alcoves for wine jugs. The

Above. Illustration from Boccaccio's *Decameron*, *c.*1435, showing a tunnel arbour or pergola constructed from coppice poles. Here several vines spread out from their bases to give complete cover.

Right. Stefano da Verona (*c.*1374 to *c.*1450), *Madonna of the rose arbour.* A coppice-pole tunnel arbour skirts the wall. Here the intermixed red and white roses give an artistic impression of the climbing *Rosa* x *alba* and the lower bush *Rosa gallica.* The Madonna, seated on a floor cushion, can lean against the bench seat which fronts the arbour in which the roses grow.

24

word arbour could imply a similar sitting place, but built of trellis work. There are also illustrations of arbours constructed from forked upright poles bearing a rafter-type roof of cross poles, over which a vine could grow (page 23). Another variation involved oak laths – thin strips split from tree trunks – and this could give an arched or even domed effect as the laths could be curved in the same way as poles (page 20).

The construction materials were available as a result of the traditional medieval method of woodland management known as 'coppice with standards'. Coppices of sprouted hazel stools were cut to the ground in rotation every ten to twenty years to supply poles of various lengths and thicknesses. Ash, alder and willow could also be coppiced. In addition such woods were planted with scattered ash and oak trees which were left uncut. The trunks grew tall and straight because the peasants were given the right to harvest any branches that they were able to remove 'by hook or by crook', with the result that long lengths of timber could be grown without knots. Forked poles were treasured. Oak laths could be vertically split from any sapling tree bole four to five feet in length (1.5 metres). Oak shingles or tiles of about nine by six inches (23 x 15 cm) could be cleft from short blocks of trunk, and twigs for tying could be harvested from one-year-old willow and hazel twigs.

This illustration from Thomas Hill's *The Gardener's Labyrinth* (1577) shows gardeners at work on the kind of tunnel arbour that seems to have been made at every period.

Drawing by the author of a fork-pole arbour constructed from ash pole uprights. Side trellises are not necessary when the vine is grown as a trunk rather than branched from the base, but are still needed for roses. Diagonal lath-work, with non-corroding copper nails at the crossings, allows the rain to run off.

26

A timber arbour of jointed carpenter's work with a plank-fronted seat in Katherine Swift's garden at Morville. Young plants of *Rosa* x *alba* are beginning to clothe the lath trellises.

Below. At Tretower Court the red *Rosa gallica* and its varieties grow to shoulder height and are useful for covering trellises which border walks.

The detailed construction of both pergolas and arbours depended on the type of plant being grown. Both of these structures could be open-sided, completely enclosed, or enclosed to shoulder height. Vines grown on a trunk do not need sides, only a roof (page 23). However vines branching sideways need trellis work from ground level, as does the climbing white *Rosa* x *alba* when grown to full height, or the sweetbriar, *Rosa rubiginosa* (page 29). But *Rosa gallica*, a red-flowering low bush, or *Rosa* x *alba*, pruned out to maintain only two to four-year-old shoots, only require shoulder-height side trellises. Illustrations commonly show both the red and white rose growing to full pergola height, but this is most probably a bit of artistic licence (page 25).

These are the only plants referred to in connection with pergolas and arbours in medieval documents, apart from bindweed, *Calystegia sepium*, which is described by William Worcestre in 1478 as twined about 'herboures', bearing white flowers resembling little church bells, which he called 'sacryingbell'. This comment suggests that there would be other acceptable plants, even the climbing bottle gourd, *Lagenaria siceriana*, being a possibility in the warm twelfth century.

Re-creating such arbours today reveals which plants might be added. The wild clematis once known as 'Virgin's Bower', *Clematis vitalba*, with

Left. Red *Rosa gallica* var. *officinalis* and white *Rosa* x *alba* 'Semiplena' growing on the tunnel arbour in Queen Eleanor's Garden, Winchester Castle.

Right. The basket work tunnel in Queen Eleanor's Garden is constructed from chestnut coppice poles, tied at the crossings. Vines, honeysuckle and red and white roses clothe the sides; ivy, pendulous sedge, ferns and Gladdon iris line the path.

its delightful form and delicate scent, must surely have been one, though from a practical point of view it is disastrous in that it periodically dies off completely. Honeysuckle, *Lonicera periclymenum*, was certainly once grown in hedges and is another obvious choice. The rambling wild bryony, *Bryonia dioica*, was well known in physic gardens and ivy is also mentioned. For ornamenting present-day versions of such a garden feature the greatest effect is given by a canopy of vines with honeysuckle twining up the end posts and the red and white roses filling in the sides.

For the shady inner borders suitable low-growing plants that would have been known in medieval gardens would be ferns such as Hart-stongue, *Phyllitis scolopendrium;* Lady fern, *Athyrium filix-femina;* and polypody, *Polypodium vulgare.* Pendulous sedge, *Carex pendula*, and greater celandine, *Chelidonium majus*, are also reliable, as is the Gladdon iris, *Iris foetidissima.* Primroses, too, thrive in the absence of dense shade in the spring. Along the lighter outer border choice is limited only by the shallow feeding roots of the vines and roses. Here violets are a first

choice. Other plants seen in trellised arbour illustrations are lily-of-the-valley, *Convallaria majalis*; Solomon's seal, *Polygonatum multiflorum*, peonies, *Paeonia mascula* and *Paeonia officinalis*, and columbine, *Aquilegia vulgaris*.

A number of questions arise in the process of re-creating these features. The problem of profile is easily solved by the countryman's advice: 'Bend the coppice poles on the ground – each type of pole will produce a different curve'. And another craftsman warned: 'Bend it when the sap is down or the poles will snap and the bark will fall off like a pair of old trousers'. How does one decide on width and height? Again this depends on the poles available, but Leonardo da Vinci was invoked for the tunnel in Queen Eleanor's Garden. One can imagine a gardener and his mate curving and tying the poles standing side by side, as well as pruning the vines and picking the grapes. Equally a king and his queen could walk arm in arm between side borders. In reality a good size is about seven feet wide by seven feet six inches high (2.1 x 2.15 metres).

What materials should be used? The most usual poles would have been hazel, willow or alder. Hazel and willow have a very short life and chestnut coppice poles, which last about ten years, have been found to be a good compromise. Children are sadly a hazard and – in the absence of village stocks – a camouflaged metal framework has proved a wise precaution in gardens which are open to the public.

Coppice-pole basket work requires tying at the crossing points. Traditionally this was done with hazel or willow withies – thin twigs twisted and bent until the cross fibres broke, giving the suppleness of string. Again it is found that in practice these require checking annually, but an almost invisible compromise is stranded fencing wire, burnt to remove the galvanised coating and soon rusted and mossed over.

Right. The entrance to the basket work tunnel arbour at Otley Hall, Suffolk. Hops act as an initial filler, increasingly replaced by the vines and roses. A mount with a spiral path beckons in the distance.

Left. Drawing by the author of a tie formed from a withy or twig of willow (or hazel). A twig of about 6mm (¼ inch) in diameter and 60-75 centimetres (2½ - 3 feet) long is bashed until the fibres are twistable. The mid-point is then looped behind the upright pole; the two ends are repeatedly crossed to form a knot and are finally wound tightly round the knot before being poked into any convenient hole to secure.

Below left. Leonardo da Vinci's famous figure (with liberties here taken by the author) is a useful conceptual tool for constructing an arch. It was used at Queen Eleanor's Garden as a guide for the re-creation of the tunnel arbour there.

Below. A detail from the painting on page 20 showing the use of withies for binding.

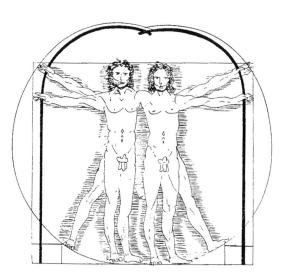

Top right. The tunnel arbour at Otley Hall on a golden evening.

Below right. A basket work arbour under construction at Otley Hall. In gardens open to the public a metal framework (to be concealed by coppice poles) gives added strength.

Left. Yew is being trained over coppice-pole arches to form a cloister at the Dower House, Morville. Beyond, a plank box seat is canopied by a carpenter's work arbour with lath trellises.

There is a good example of this type of tunnel pergola in Queen Eleanor's Garden in Winchester (page 29). At Otley Hall near Ipswich there is a magnificent 90 foot (27 metre) tunnel as well as trellised arbours. These carefully researched and executed re-creations make it still possible to walk in a medieval garden redolent of medieval times on a sultry day and experience Froissart's pleasure in stepping into a tunnel arbour, 'pleasant and shady and covered in vines'.

JAN WOUDSTRA

Bowers, 'Berceaux' and Cradle Walks

The formal garden featured in this British portrait of William Langley, *c.*1636, is surrounded by a covered walkway typical of the gardens of the period as illustrated by Hans Vredeman de Vries (see page 40).

While rustic pergolas as we know them were common during the renaissance and baroque era, garden writers rarely referred to them, preferring to discuss more elaborate structures instead. John Evelyn even noted: 'Pergulas are also such bowers as are covered with vines frequent in every garden; therefore we passe them over here briefly'.

Much was made by contemporary authors of the difference between a bower and an arbour, the former generally referring to a covered walk or tunnel and the latter to a smaller structure emulating a built form, but this distinction was not always maintained and the terms were frequently interchanged. Several other words were also used; contemporary authors wrote of tunnels or cradle work. The latter is a direct translation of the French *berceau* and refers to the elaborate wooden framework. It was the word most often used for this feature in European gardens. Another French term is *charmille* after *charme* or hornbeam (*Carpinus betulus*), which was the most popular plant for bowers in the late seventeenth and eighteenth century when seasonal and climbing plants were becoming less fashionable.

These elaborate structures were key elements in European renaissance and baroque gardens; they both strengthened the geometry and provided an iconographical reference. Sometimes they were used to highlight a particular feature and provide a focus, sometimes they determined the extent of space and formed cloister-like enclosures, and sometimes they could give directional guidance. They were also intended to provide shelter from sun and wind.

The basic design was a framework of curved or semicircular shape over which plants were grown. During the sixteenth century the structures were of timber and mainly planted with annual or woody climbers. It was during the early seventeenth century that they were for the first time covered permanently with hedge-like vegetation, and this became the general rule by the end of the century. At this time highly elaborate structures appeared in gardens like stage sets, with sections built with an iron framework. They were not intended to be covered by plants, but to be appreciated for their architectural merit alone. In eighteenth-century baroque gardens there were often both the so-called 'natural' plant-covered arbours and bowers and 'artificial' ones.

Art historians generally consider Francesco Colonna's *Hypnerotomachia Poliphili* (1499) describing Poliphilo's dream enacted in a garden as an important introduction to the Renaissance. This book was widely published, both in its original Latin and translated into French. The illustrations depict the various scenes and include garden structures which clearly relate to both medieval and classical examples. They were covered in roses of various colours and with jasmine, honeysuckle, privet and wild vines. Both the illustrations and descriptions were a source of inspiration for garden architects.

Despite the hot and sunny climate, shady tunnels did not become popular features in Italian gardens. There were examples at Petraia and L'Ambrogiana which were extensive and created separate garden areas, each incorporating four compartments (pages 38-39). Yet architecturally they were relatively simple affairs without ornamentation, in contrast to that at the Villa d'Este in Tivoli. This had an elaborate cross-shaped structure in the centre of the flat lower part of the garden, with separate pavilions in the four squares thus formed. Observed and engraved by the French architect Etienne du Perac in 1573, this was the type of structure which was to become famous in France through the work of another architect, Androuet du Cerceau. The latter designed and engraved some magnificent examples during the second half of the sixteenth century in his widely influential *Les plus excellents bastiments de France* (1576-79).

At Montargis two elaborate architectural tunnel arbours were placed opposite the entrance to the castle. They were tapered towards the entrance, thus forming an impressive directional structure. They were covered with ivy but contemporary illustrations show the bare timber framework. At Blois one arbour was conceived in a cruciform like that at Tivoli, while another formed a gallery surrounding a compartmented garden. A third ran between two walls, while there were also separate corner pavilions. Blois shows some of the many ways these structures might be used.

It is clear that all these creations were planted, but so far there is only information for the planting at Montargis. Contemporary horticultural

Above. Francesco Colonna's *Hypnerotomachia Poliphili* went through various editions and depicted a range of garden structures. Here one from the 1546 French edition *Le Songe de Polyphile* shows a clear relationship with classical examples.

Left. An engraving entitled *Spring* from a painting by Peter Breughel the Elder (1565) shows the seasonal work of tying and pruning climbers. The structure itself is a timber construction with carved entrance pillars.

Details from Du Cerceau's engravings of Montargis (*right*) and Blois (*below*). They show bare timber, but we know that the structure at Montargis was covered with ivy.

DEAMBVLATIONI
NVNC HEDER

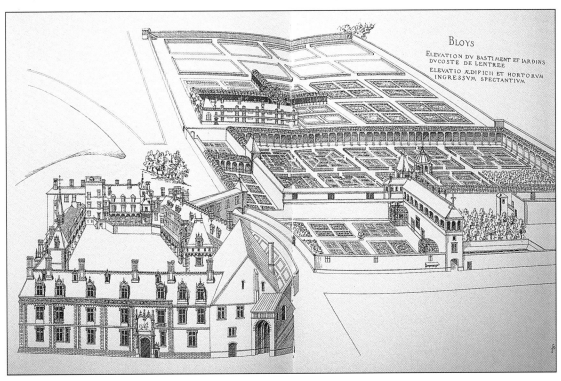

BLOYS

ELEVATION DV BASTIMENT ET IARDINS
DV COSTE DE L'ENTREE
ELEVATIO ÆDIFICII ET HORTORVM
INGRESSVM SPECTANTIVM

literature fills this gap. Charles Estienne initially based his writing on classical sources, but he elaborated on those with his son-in-law Jean Liébault in *L'agriculture et maison rustique*; an extended 1570 edition discusses parterres surrounded by *berceaux* covered with jasmine (*Jasminum officinale*), scau notre dame (*Tamus communis*), musk roses (*Rosa moschata*) and other special plants. Estienne notes that a pergola type trellis ('in the shape of an *auvent*') provides an alternative in kitchen gardens, because *berceaux* are too expensive to maintain. These pergolas are constructed of oak posts, charred where they enter the soil, and juniper poles. They are planted with vines, which are renewed every five years. The 1622 edition of *Maison rustique* adds to this, suggesting that any plants which are flexible and create shade with their foliage are suitable. The list includes bryony (*Bryonia dioica*), hops (*Humulus lupulus*), a climbing variety of courgette (*Cucurbita pepo*) and cucumber (*Cucumis sativus / C. anguiria*), everlasting pea (*Lathyrus latifolius*), coquerelles (the name now given to *Physalis alkegengi* but whose size and habit makes it an unlikely choice for a bower) and pomme de merveilles (*Cucumis melo*, possibly the cultivar 'Dudaim'). This last is considered the best to plant over a *berceau* because it is beautiful, flexible and will trail easily over the structure. As this group are all perennials or annuals, the structure would be bare in winter.

Olivier de Serres in *Le théâtre d'agriculture* (1600) also mentions the pomme de merveilles as suitable for tunnels and, remarkably, he adds love apples (or tomatoes) and pommes dorées (possibly oranges). A further list of plants for shade cabinets, bowers and trellis work includes plants with flexible branches and fruit trees, such as hazel (*Corylus avellana*), cherry (*Prunus avium*), mulberry (*Morus nigra*), pomegranate (*Punica granatum*); evergreens such as the olive (*Olea europaea*), pine (*Pinus* sp.), and, in the south near the Mediterranean, orange (*Citrus aurantium*) and lemon trees (*Citrus limon*). He considers the cypress (*Cupressus sempervirens*) and bay (*Laurus nobilis*) the best trees. The only climber referred to in this section is the vine (*Vitis vinifera*). Another remarkable addition to this list is the small savin (*Juniperus sabina*), while ivy (*Hedera helix*) is a more obvious choice, as are hops (*Humulus lupu-*

lus) and honeysuckle (*Lonicera* sp.). These lists do highlight the amazing variety of plants proposed.

In England too there was a particular interest in seasonal plants for garden structures. John Gerard in *The Herball* (1633) follows the example of Estienne and Liébault in recommending annual climbers, such as gourd and wild gourd. The latter is a variety of *Cucurbita pepo* which 'clymbeth upon Arbours and banquetting houses'. There is also reference to woody climbers, like the various jasmines (*Jasminum* spp.) and Ladies bower or Virgins bower (*Clematis viticella*). Gerard thought the common name of the latter to derive 'from its aptnesse in making Arbors, Bowers, and shadie covertures in gardens'.

A quite different approach was taken with the planting of the tunnel arbour in the Tuileries for Henry IV. The garden had been destroyed when he entered Paris in 1594 and was finally restored *circa* 1600, by Claude Mollet, presumably under the supervision of Etienne du Perac, who had been appointed Architecte du Roi in 1595. Mollet and du Perac had previously worked together at Anet and at St Germain-en-Laye and had been instrumental in various innovations in garden design. At Anet they had introduced the parterre de broderie in the 1580s and in 1595 at St Germain they used labour-saving box for the first time to delineate the parterres. At the Tuileries a *berceau* was included on the north side and was extended between 1609 and 1615 to the whole length of the garden, some 600 metres (2000 feet) in length and 4.5 metres (15 feet) wide. It was built in the same style as the one at Tivoli and contemporary illustrations show it as a timber structure. Yet in his posthumously published *Théâtre des plans et jardinages* (1652) Claude Mollet notes that elms, and particularly female elms (*Ulmus procera* var.), are the best plants for covering *berceaux*, which appears consistent with his search for more permanent and less labour intensive and thus cheaper plantings. This type of permanently planted *berceau* appears to have reached its extreme in the gardens at Liancourt laid out after 1620 and depicted by Mauperché in 1654. This shows tunnels throughout and around various garden areas and must have been a maintenance nightmare. It is perhaps not surprising that by 1687 the gardens were ill kept.

Detail of a lunette depicting the garden at Ambrogiana by Giusto Utens (1599). It shows one of the few tunnel arbours known to have been built in Italian Renaissance gardens.

En genus humanū Deus et Natura creatrix,
Mollibus e cunis, grauidag parentis ab aluo,.

.I.
COMPOSITA.

Ducit ad ærumnas, his mollibus educat vmbris,
Illos fortuna iubet incufare potentem.

Left. An engraving from Hans Vredeman de Vries's widely influential *Hortorum viridiarumque…*, Antwerp 1587, which shows the kind of garden architecture now often associated with renaissance gardens.

Right. Isaac Oliver's *Portrait of a melancholy young man,* c.1590-95, shows a heavy timber structure surrounding a garden and relates clearly to continental renaissance examples, such as those engraved by Hans Vredeman de Vries.

The development of this feature reached its apogee in The Netherlands where the tradition was illustrated in the engravings of Jan Vredeman de Vries in *Hortorum viridiarumque* (1587). These show a variety of tunnels, bowers and arbours related to architectural styles. They were intended for smaller gardens and were mostly planted with what appear to be climbers. The structures clearly provided entrance points and central architectural features and some made cloister gardens with shady sheltered walks. This tradition was continued by Crispin van de Passe in *Hortus floridus* (1615), and there are recorded examples. A remarkable one was laid out at Het Buitenhof in The Hague for Prince Maurits in the early seventeenth century and consisted of two tunnel arbours connected by a central pavilion.

Below. The garden at Het Buitenhof in The Hague was remarkable for its complicated structures and elaborate decoration, evidence of which survives on contemporary engravings and in a 1623 description.

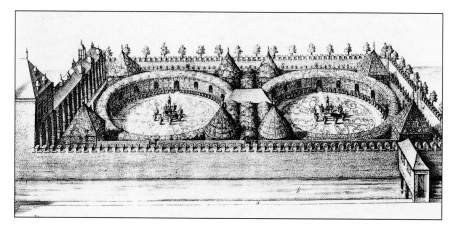

Francis Bacon appears to be referring to the Dutch tradition when he describes his ideal garden in his essay 'Of Gardens' (1625). He suggests one might 'Plant a *Covert Alley,* upon Carpenters Worke, about Twelve Foot in Height, by which you may goe in Shade, into the Garden'. There was to be a square garden:

Incompassed, on all the Foure Sides, with a *Stately Arched Hedge.* The *Arches* to be upon *Pillars,* of Carpenters Worke, of some Ten Foot high, and Six Foot broad: And the *Spaces* between, of the same Dimension, with the *Breadth* of the *Arch.* Over the *Arches,* let there bee an *Entire Hedge,* of some Four Foote High, framed also upon Carpenters Worke: And upon the *Upper Hedge,* over every *Arch,* a little *Turret,* with a *Belly,* enough to receive a *Cage* of *Birds:* And over every *Space,* betweene the *Arches,* some other little *Figure,* with Broad Plates of *Round Coloured Glasse,* gilt, for the *Sunne,* to Play upon. But this *Hedge* I intend to be, raised upon a *Bancke,* not Steepe, but gently Slope, of some Six Foot, set all with *Flowers.*

Records of British examples of such structures, however, are scarce, but there were two along either side of the garden at Wilton designed by Salomon de Caus, *circa* 1645. Neither of these was described in detail, but John Evelyn also proposes an ideal garden structure in his *Elysium Britannicum* which was to be the same twelve feet high as Bacon's. He does not specify the width but he notes elsewhere that a 'covered walk must be much narrower than the open'. This was for the same aesthetic reasons as those proposed by Jacques Boyceau in his *Traité du jardinage* (1638), when he noted that a covered walk looked wider than an open walk and thus should be designed to narrower proportions.

Evelyn's design was to be constructed of cleft oak. Cleft oak would have given a surface more resistant to rot than sawn. The horizontal rails were to be spiked (nailed) or pinned together. Evelyn also provided information about a cheaper and less solid construction using sweet chestnut or ash poles. While they did not last very long they could easily be repaired. The height and width was to be proportional to that of the walk and the design dependent on the habit and speed of growth of the plant material used to cover it. He considered hornbeam the most suitable for well-covered bowers, but that elm and field maple

might also be used. Tall, straight, well-furnished plants should be chosen for the purpose and planted at one foot spacings. In 1664 Evelyn referred to the hornbeam bowers in the Luxembourg gardens in Paris and at Hampton Court as good examples. The bower at Hampton Court finally made way for another when William and Mary altered the gardens in 1689.

The new bower (it has always been called a bower) on the terrace in the Privy Garden at Hampton Court was approximately 90 metres (100 yards) long. Detailed research has revealed that it was originally 3.6 metres (12 feet wide) and 5.4 metres (18 feet) high. It was constructed from oak uprights and fir rails, with the uprights placed on top of two sill beams which supported the structure. There was an opening in the centre which lined up with the new garden. The bower was painted verdigris green with gilding on both fronts, and was planted with wych elm on a 1.2 metre (4 foot) spacing. The timber structure gradually deteriorated and was removed, but the elms survived until the 1970s when they succumbed to Dutch elm disease. The bower was immediately

Above and right. **The recently recreated Queen Mary's Bower in the Privy Garden at Hampton Court.**

Below. **The bower at the Queen's Garden at Het Loo was built of oak and was 12½ feet wide and 20 feet high (3.75 x 6.00 metres) with arched openings or windows each 5½ feet wide (1.65 metres). It contained built-in aviaries for exotic birds.**

replaced with a modern one, which in turn was removed when the gardens were reconstructed in 1995. The present copy of the historic bower is planted with hornbeam rather than elm.

The original bower at Hampton Court may have been constructed by the same team as made the one in the Queen's Garden at Het Loo in The Netherlands. This was designed by Hans Willem Bentinck, William III's advisor, in 1688, and bears a strong resemblance to his own bower at Zorgvliet. It is also very similar to a design by Daniel Marot, who also worked at Het Loo at this time. A well covered *berceau* surrounds a square plot with little turrets at the corners; there is an opening at the centre of the sides and arched openings or windows over the whole length. As in the garden in Bacon's essay there were exotic birds in aviaries specially built within the trellis.

The royal English gardeners George London and Henry Wise wrote about these structures, referred to as galleries, arcades and porticoes, under the heading of Hornbeam. This was because their book *The Retir'd Gard'ner* (1706) was a translation from the French where such features were then often referred to as *charmille* (after hornbeam). Yet they noted that in England lime trees were used for covering 'Portico-Galleries', by

which they appear to understand arched tunnels with openings or windows cut in one of the sides. A second description of this feature comes under the heading of Elm tree, where an alternative construction method is explained of first training a tall straight tree, and then tying an arch into it and leading the branches over it. The smaller features are normally properly constructed as joiner's work and painted green. *Phillyrea*, one of the most popular evergreen shrubs in the seventeenth and eighteenth centuries, is a favourite plant to cover them. Properly made carpenter's work might not always be affordable and they suggest an alternative: 'Willow-tree or some other good Wood, which they fasten to each other with Osier or Wire to put them into the Form that suits them best'.

The general reasons for providing these structures in gardens were well expressed by John Worlidge in his garden treatise *Systema horti-culturae* (1677). He noted:

To make a Garden pleasant at all times and in all seasons, either in respect of the great variety of Weather, or your own disposition or indisposition, it will be very necessary to accommodate it with places of shade, to skreen you from the scorching Sun-Beams, Canopies to preserve you from the Rain, and Boxes to seclude you from the too cold Breezes.

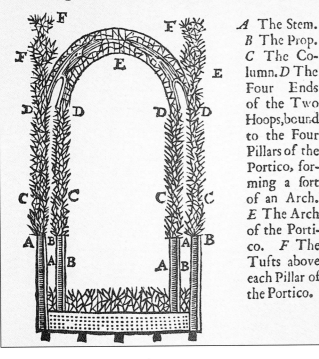

This Obſervation, which is very important, duly minded, and the Four Columns rais'd to an equal height, propp'd up by Poles, and rais'd as high as they ſhould be, you take the Hoops, as I have hinted before, and tie them one upon another, in the form of a Half-Moon, on the Columns, by which means you make a ſort of an Arch in the Middle, and that is your Portico.

Upon each Column there will appear a Tuft of Branches, cut in the form of an Apple, and a little piked at the End, which is a great helps to Works of this Nature. But that your Idea of it may be the more lively, I ſhall here repreſent the Figure of a Portico without Leaves, wherein you will ſee all the Parts of which 'tis compos'd.

The Figure of a Portico without Leaves.

A The Stem. *B* The Prop. *C* The Column. *D* The Four Ends of the Two Hoops, bound to the Four Pillars of the Portico, forming a ſort of an Arch. *E* The Arch of the Portico. *F* The Tufts above each Pillar of the Portico.

These garden structures did not always receive a good press and also had disadvantages, once again aptly expressed by Worlidge. They require much maintenance; they are moist, foul and cold, and thus impair the health; and they drip after a shower long after the rain has stopped. He preferred a shady lime or plane tree, rather than 'to be hood-winked in an Arbour'. Despite these negative comments and despite the fact that they were re-iterated by other influential authors, such as Philip Miller, the curator of the Chelsea Physic Garden in his *Gardeners Dictionary* (1731), there were many such features in gardens, both then and later.

During the last quarter of the seventeenth century French gardens developed these structures primarily as architectural features made of lattice work supported by an ironwork frame. André le Nôtre (possibly assisted by the architect Mansart) designed such features at Versailles, Chantilly, Grand Trianon, Chaville, and Sceaux, where they provided a décor or a front to a *berceau*. Since they were not intended to support plants they were referred to as 'artificial' by A.C.Daviler, in his *Cours d'architecture* (1691). He provided general rules for the proportions of *berceaux*. The height was to be one third more than the width and the arch should not be an exact semicircle, but the centre point should be lowered to achieve perfection, as at Sceaux. Dézallier d'Argenville adopted this classification of artificial and natural in *La théorie et la pratique du jardinage* (1709), as translated by John James in *The Theory and Practice of Gardening* (1713). Natural arbours were formed 'only by the Branches of Trees artfully interwoven, and sustain'd by strong Lattice-work, Hoops, Poles, &c'. These were planted with female elms, Dutch lime trees, with hornbeams to fill up the lower parts. Artificial ones were:

made wholly of Lattice-work, supported by Standards, Cross-rails, Circles and Arches of Iron. For this purpose they make use of Fillets of Oak, somewhat more than an Inch square every way, which being well plained and made strait, are wrought into Checkers of six or seven Inches square, and fasten'd together with Iron-Wire. They make use likewise of Wainscot for the Moldings and Ornaments of Cornices, and of Quarter-Stuff for large Plinths and Facias.

Left. The recreated tunnel walkway at Moseley Old Hall, Staffordshire, was based on seventeenth-century illustrations.

Above and right. The restored ironwork at Schönbrunn and the dramatic silhouettes of the bare trees that were grown over the original simple arches at this palace in Vienna.

Near left and right. The construction of the hornbeam tunnel round the Cherry Garden at Ham House is based on the assumption that these were a feature of late seventeenth-century gardens rather than on documentary or archaeological evidence.

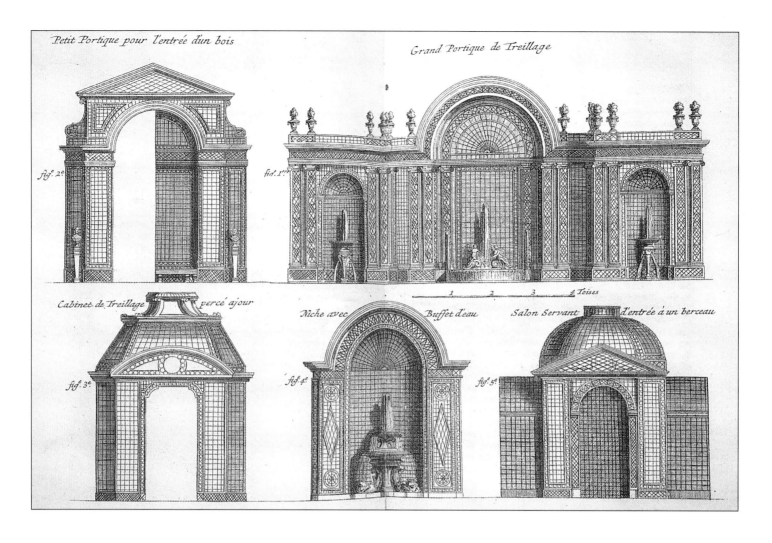

Petit Portique pour l'entrée d'un bois

Grand Portique de Treillage

fig. 2.^e

fid. 1.re

Cabinet de Treillage percé à jour

fig. 3.^e

Niche avec ...... Buffet d'eau

fig. 4.^e

Salon Servant ...... d'entrée à un berceau

fig. 5.^e

1   2   3   4 Toises

He noted how in cities such features might be used to terminate a garden, to obscure a wall or an undesirable feature. Otherwise they served well as a focal point, and when made into niches for seats or statues, they were often covered with roses, honeysuckles, jasmines and wild vines (*Tamus communis*).

The most detailed advice on the construction of artificial bowers was given by M.Roubo in his *L'art du treillageur ou menuiserie des jardins* (1775). This noted the existence of a separate profession of *Treillageurs* (Trellis makers). Since the time of Louis XIV trellis workers had not suffered from changes in fashion, but designs had generally become more complicated. Elaborate structures continued to be built in eighteenth-century French gardens either of timber or with an iron frame supported by masonry or special braces, with the rest made of wooden latticework tied together to provide rigidity. Oak was the preferred timber for structural work, and for

trelliswork sweet chestnut, oak and ash, with alternatives including alder, birch, cypress, bay, white mulberry, pine, *Celtis australis* and willow, when other options were not available. Metal wire and nails were recommended to hold it firmly together.

Examples of French artificial arbours were readily adopted in publications in other countries, as in Batty Langley's *New Principles of Gardening* (1728), and examples of these continued to be found in eighteenth-century baroque gardens, in, for example, Germany or Austria. In most instances they formed a section at the end of or within a natural bower, as at Belvedere and Schön-brunn in Vienna.

Arbours and bowers have been particularly identified with renaissance and baroque gardens and as they have romantic associations, they have been favourite features in nineteenth and twentieth-century reconstructions. So much have they been identified with gardens of this period

Garden structures and trellis continued to be popular in French gardens during the eighteenth century when M.Roubo reported that the only change was that they had become more complicated. Two illustrations from A.J.Roubo's 1775 *L'Art du treillageur ou menuiserie des jardins* (manual on the art of treillage). The great detail shown allows accurate reconstructions to be made.

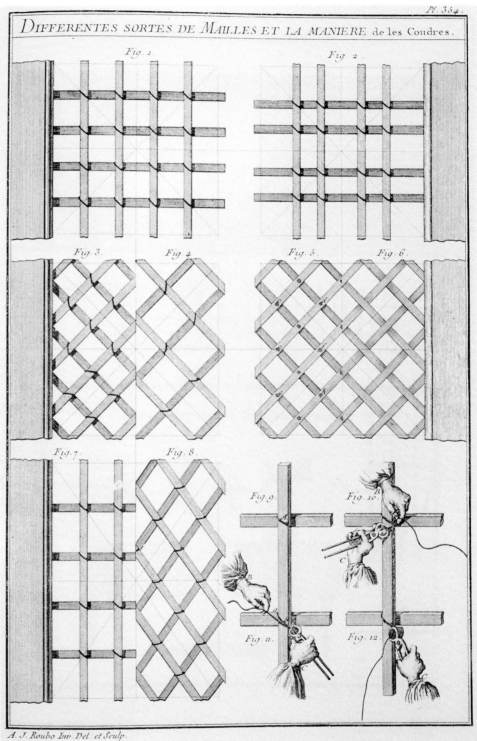

that even where there was no evidence that there was ever such a feature, pastiche versions have appeared, as at Ham House, where the gardens were reconstructed in the 1970s. There are also such examples in the gardens of Williamsburg reconstructed in the 1930s. This shows how the glamorous reputation of these features has far exceeded the evidence, and that, as in the early renaissance era, their creators have once more been inspired by literature and art.

ROBIN WHALLEY

Victorian Rose Gardens and Arts and Crafts Pergolas

The pergolas that became such popular features of English gardens in the early twentieth century owed their immediate origins to examples found in Italy. Before then Regency and Victorian gardeners grew their climbers freely over arches and arbours, revelling in the new opportunities offered by ironwork frames and the ever-increasing number of available plants.

There had been few if any such structures during the Georgian era when the English landscape garden reigned supreme, but towards the end of Humphry Repton's highly successful career as a landscape gardener (1752-1818) he began writing and publishing graphic accounts of his methods and designs. Some of the ornamental flowery features which so characterised Regency gardens began to appear in his later work. At his own garden at Hare Street in Essex, he transformed the view on to the village high street with flowering climbers on the trees and an iron frame on the lawn supporting a vase of roses. At Ashridge in Hertfordshire he designed a circular rose garden and surrounded it with a light arcade supporting climbing roses (see over).

As the century progressed, and with it an increasing obsession with roses and confidence with iron, structures like these became more and more popular. In *The Rose Garden* (1848) William

Previous pages, page 50.
The rustic pergola at Great Tangley Manor, near Guildford, Surrey. The garden was designed by Philip Webb in 1865 to marry with the sixteenth-century half-timbered house. Webb was one of William Morris's closest colleagues and his work epitomises the Arts and Crafts style.

Previous pages, page 51.
The restored late nineteenth-century metalwork arbour now outside the dairy at Waddesdon Manor, Buckinghamshire.

Left above. Repton's own aquatint of the rosarium at Ashridge as it appeared in his *Fragments on the Theory and Practice of Landscape Gardening* in 1816. He designed it *circa* 1812 for the Earl of Bridgewater.

Left. Valleyfield, Fife, was illustrated in Repton's *Observations on the Theory and Practice of Landscape Gardening* which was published in 1803.

The English architect Cecil Pinsent designed the gardens at La Foce in Tuscany for Iris Origo between 1924 and 1939. The collaboration between English and American garden designers and the owners of grand Italian villas in the first half of the twentieth century led to the increasing popularity of the pergola in British and American gardens.

A photograph taken in 1936 of Lord Brownlow and his family in the grand ironwork arcade at Belton.

Paul suggested a similar but larger circular rosarium with climbing roses on arches. At Trentham between 1834 and 1842 the gardener George Fleming covered a long arched walk of iron hoops stretching down the east side of the Italian gardens with roses, honeysuckles and clematis. The hoops are still there today. A similarly simple structure was later used for the laburnum tunnel at Bodnant (see page 91). In the second half of the nineteenth century an elaborate circular arcaded structure in iron was erected at Belton in Lincolnshire. It is yet another example of the all-pervading fashion for rose arches, arbours and covered walks so characteristic of the Victorian rose garden.

Yet there is no mention of the word 'pergola' in the garden literature of mid Victorian England, nor indeed any reference until the late nineteenth century to the kind of structures which compare so closely with the pergolas of Italy. Changes in garden design began to surface around 1870, taking their inspiration from traditional English gardens. The writer E.V.Boyle developed schemes for the 'old fashioned garden' and, significantly, in *Days and Hours in a Garden* (1884) she suggested

Above. Another view of La Foce showing the wisteria clad pergola.

Right. William Robinson's own garden at Gravetye has been restored. The white wisteria clad pergola is a reminder of his enthusiasm for this feature.

the use of a '*pergola*' for climbing roses, but she put the word in italics suggesting how new it was. Here the word referred to the simple rustic pergolas of the Italian country villa rather than the ornate trellis walks and arcades of the Renaissance. Perhaps it is no coincidence that a growing enthusiasm for the pergola ran parallel to a revival of interest in the villa gardens of Italy, stimulated by more English and American visits to Italy. Charles Platt's *Italian Gardens* (1894) and Edith Wharton's *Italian Villas and their Gardens* (1904) were both received with great acclaim.

Although the garden writer William Robinson (1838-1935) is chiefly associated with his antagonism to the formal garden and his pronouncements in favour of the wild garden, he was, surprisingly, one of the earliest to draw attention to the potential of the Italian pergola for shaded walks and climbing plants. In the second edition of the *English Flower Garden* (1889) he wrote:

Adaptations of the Italian pergola are much to be recommended in English gardens, for though our summer is short, there are a good three months when a bowery shaded walk would be most enjoyable, and besides Vines, the numbers of free-growing climbing plants at our disposal give an abundant choice of material. Aristolochia, Wistaria, Virginian Creeper,

rambling Roses, Honeysuckles, Jasmines, and the free clematises are all suitable, and both look well and do well in such a position.

He includes an illustration captioned: 'An Italian Pergola, or Creeper-clad Covered Way, in the old Capuchin Convent at Amalfi, Southern Italy'. This particular pergola, high up on the hillside above Amalfi looking out over the Gulf of Salerno, was to become an icon for the English vision of the Italian pergola, appearing widely in the works of the renowned gardener, Gertrude Jekyll (1843-1932). Robinson in his references to pergolas was only concerned with the trabeated structure of upright stone, masonry or oak pillars supporting rough stems of oak laid horizontally across the top. The subject of pergolas continued to gain ground in later editions of the *English Flower Garden* with examples of both masonry columns and more rustic wooden versions. Again a

The influential illustration of the pergola at the Capuchin monastery in Amalfi as reproduced in the second edition of Robinson's *The English Flower Garden.*

The simple vine-covered willow pole pergola in Gertrude Jekyll's sister's garden in Venice as illustrated in *The English Flower Garden* (1893). The combination of covered pergola and Madonna lilies below was much copied in England.

Right. Gertrude Jekyll's pergola newly built in her own garden at Munstead Wood. The illustration featured without attribution in the third edition of Robinson's *The English Flower Garden.*

particularly favoured example appears in the third edition (1893): in place of the Capuchin monastery there is a view of white lilies growing under a simple rustic wooden pergola in Mrs Eden's garden in Venice. In its rustic simplicity this example would have appealed to Robinson and furthermore, Gertrude Jekyll, who wrote regularly for Robinson's publication, *The Garden*, was Mrs Eden's sister. It is no surprise then that Gertrude Jekyll, who stayed with her sister in Venice during her formative years, herself became a great advocate of the pergola and by 1902 was writing in *The Garden*:

It is only of comparatively late years that we have borrowed the pergola from the gardens of Italy. Borrowed is perhaps, in its complete sense, not quite the right term to use, for borrowing implies returning or repaying, whereas, having borrowed the pergola, we have certainly kept it for our own.

57

The Manor house at Upton Grey is one of the few gardens where Gertrude Jekyll's planting plans survive and have been used as the basis of re-creation. Here a rope hung pergola is festooned in the richly flowering 'Dundee Rambler'.

Later in *Garden Ornament* (1918) Jekyll continued with her praise for 'a feature that has added so greatly to the beauty and interest of our pleasure grounds'. She was enthusiastic about the use of pergolas in other gardens of the period, particularly in the examples by the landscape architect, Harold Peto (1854-1933), in gardens in the south of France. These had pergolas similar in style to the pergola he created at West Dean in Sussex (see pages 97-101). Jekyll also covered treillage in *Garden Ornament* and included Peto's garden at Easton Lodge (see over) among her illustrations.

At her own garden at Munstead Wood she built a pergola as a shaded walk leading to the long border, and in her plan for the small garden at Millmead, Bramley, she designed a pergola to make a covered way leading round the house from the front garden to the back.

The architect Edwin Lutyens (1869-1944), who formed a partnership with Gertrude Jekyll on many garden commissions, designed one of the earliest classical style pergolas at Woodside, Buckinghamshire, as early as 1893 with uprights of Doric columns arranged in pairs around a pond.

Right. The garden at Hestercombe is an outstanding example of the collaboration between Gertrude Jekyll and Edwin Lutyens. The use of local stone for terraces, steps, paths and pillars gives an overall unity to an ambitious scheme.

Left. Two photographs from *Country Life* of one of the magnificent pergolas at Easton Lodge designed by Harold Peto for the Countess of Warwick in 1902. They collapsed under snow in 1922 and all that remains is one *Periploca graeca* now clambering right up into a tree.

The fine traditional tunnel arbour at Knole in Kent as photographed in about 1865. Like so many of these timber structures it has vanished without trace.

Many of Lutyens's gardens used pergolas with brilliant effect and they often display careful detailing of materials and constructional forms as at Hestercombe in Somerset (see pages 79-83).

Almost in parallel with the writings of Boyle and Robinson was the formation of the Arts and Crafts movement, which grew out of the Art Workers' Guild which began life in 1884. It was this movement which sought to bring art and craft together with its all-embracing attitude to architecture and garden design. In general the Arts and Crafts movement espoused English traditions and in landscape design sought, like E.V.Boyle, to restore to favour the old gardens of England, which had so often been destroyed by the fashion for landscape gardening in the eighteenth century. Despite this desire for Englishness the Arts and Crafts architects happily adopted the Italian pergola, rather than the characteristic English bower, and it appears that by the beginning of the twentieth century no garden design by the leading Arts and Crafts architects was complete without a pergola. One of their stated aims was to marry house

and garden and nowhere is this more clearly expressed than in the writings of William Morris (1834-96):

And now to sum up as to a garden… It should by no means imitate either the wilfulness or the wildness of Nature, but should look like a thing never to be seen except near a house.

Many of the movement's architects followed this principle of design (particularly Edward Prior, Robert Shultz, Charles Mallows and Baillie Scott) and the pergola with its elemental built structure of post and beam and covering of vegetation obviously provided them with a perfect way of uniting house and garden. In one of the leading books of the Arts and Crafts movement, *The Formal Garden in England* (1892) Reginald Blomfield set out their view of the English garden, making some significant references to pergolas by stressing their Italian origin, but also recognising their importance as suitable structures for climbing plants. Later Edward Prior, in his article 'Garden-Making' in the *Studio* (1901) emphasised the simplicity of the

Left. The simple but effective brick and timber pergola at Barrington Court where Gertrude Jekyll planned the flower garden. Now owned by the National Trust the garden is undergoing a complete restoration.

Above. A watercolour by Enest Arthur Rowe (1863-1922) called *The Rose Pergola, Blackhurst House, Tunbridge Wells, Kent*. The painting perfectly captures the period romance of a long rustic rose covered pergola.

A detail of one of many plans by Inigo Triggs, author of *Formal Gardens in England and Scotland* (1902), in which a pergola is a prominent feature. Mawson wrote: 'Pergolas ... are required in almost every garden'.

pergola, which he described as being constructed of 'rough sawn deal or larch poles'.

Another enormously influential book to be published at this time was Mawson's *The Art and Craft of Garden Making*, which appeared in five editions between 1900 and 1926. This book differed very much from the approach of Blomfield – it was a clearly written explanation of the making of gardens, but at the same time included many examples of his own work. Thomas Mawson (1861-1933), who became widely sought after as a garden designer and took on many commissions during the Edwardian period, was very well aware of the Arts and Crafts vogue. In style his work stemmed from the English formal garden, but at the same time gave it the practicality for use with the modern house and smaller gardens of the period. With the new vogue for pergolas in garden design it is not surprising that the first edition of his book (1900) includes them among its garden features:

Arbours and pergolas are both features which lend a peculiar charm to a garden, affording delightful shade in hot weather, and when covered with suitable climbers such as Clematis montana, or Honeysuckles, forming a retreat which it will ever be a delight to visit and rest under.

He continues with brief and simple guidance for their construction, but includes no examples of pergolas in his sample plans at the end of the book. However by the time of the fourth edition in 1912 the section on pergolas has been greatly augmented, running to several pages, and he stipulates: 'Pergolas...are required in almost every garden...a pergola is invaluable', and: 'There is almost unlimited scope for originality in the planning and designs of pergolas'. Nothing could speak more clearly of the growing ubiquity of pergolas in the first decade of the twentieth century. Mawson's garden schemes more often than not included pergolas, some on a truly grand scale as the one at

The long pergola at Nymans in Sussex is massively built in stone with timber beams. It was put up in 1903 and planted with *Wisteria floribunda* 'Macrobotrys' brought over from the Wada nursery in Japan in 1904.

The Hill, Hampstead, which was constructed in three phases over many years from about 1905 to1920 (see pages 84-89).

Although the use of pergolas continued during the twentieth century, remaining both in name and type a common feature of our gardens, arguably no others were built to the same scale and style as those of the Arts and Crafts period. One fine example created just after the First World War was the one built at Great Fosters in Surrey by the partnership of Romaine-Walker and Jenkins (see pages 104-107), where they set out to create 'such a garden as would re-create the old-world charm of the place and be interesting the year round'. A pergola was by then an essential aspiration for such a design.

A N D R E W   C L A Y D E N

Pergolas of Today and Tomorrow

An arbour in its most, organic, dynamic and sustainable form. Two photographs of the living willow structure at the Heeley Millennium Park in Sheffield.

The pergola was once a thing of beauty, hand-crafted and unique. Unfortunately this cannot be said for all modern interpretations, which like so many garden features have been manufactured for the convenience of the quick fix garden, available off the shelf, and installed before Sunday lunch. Fortunately there are still fine examples to be seen in many private gardens and public landscapes. These are the products of ambitious clients and designers who recognise the full potential of these structures and understand how they can contribute to their designs both functionally and aesthetically.

This chapter looks to review a limited selection of contemporary examples. These challenge the convention of a timber or metal structure located in a garden setting. Instead all are taken from the public realm and are the designs of landscape architects, architects and environmental artists. They represent a range of ideas which start

at the human scale of living willow structures and organic forms sculpted in green oak, and progress towards the eye-catching and dramatic steel and stainless steel sculptures where any additional adornment by climbing plants would be an intrusion. They also demonstrate how, if these features are designed with care and imagination, their unique qualities can enrich a scheme beyond the mere function of a framework on which climbing plants may grow.

The first example is a living willow structure that was designed by Mandy Burton and Lee Furness with local schoolchildren for the Heeley Millennium Park in Sheffield. This arbour was created from willow wands (single branches up to 3 metres [10 feet] in length), which were pushed into the ground and then woven and tied into place. At least 30-45 centimetres (12-18 inches) of the willow must be inserted into the ground in the dormant season and then kept well watered in spring and summer in order to encourage root growth. In this example a slender steel frame has been incorporated in the structure to provide additional support; this should not be necessary in a private garden. Over time the structure will become stronger as the willow wands establish and the tied stems fuse together. This must surely be an example of an arbour in its most organic, dynamic and sustainable form. Because the method of construction is a low tech solution there are real opportunities to involve the local community in the design, construction and ongoing maintenance. There are a wide range of different willow varieties to choose from including the bright orange stemmed scarlet willow (*Salix alba* 'Britzensis') and the purple and white bloomed violet willow (*Salix daphnoides*). Like a topiary hedge, there are also exciting opportunities for the feature to be extended and reshaped in subsequent years. Before the growing season starts the

previous summer's growth should be pruned or woven back into the structure. This regular maintenance will encourage the new growth which has the most intensive colour. Living willow can also be used to construct a wide range of other garden features including sculptures and fences. Willow fences can be particularly effective in providing shelter and support for herbaceous plants and also have the advantage of good light penetration in the early part of the growing season.

The next example is taken from the Earth Centre in South Yorkshire; a visitor attraction which seeks to promote long term environmental sustainability. Designers working on the project are required to produce designs that follow this guiding principle. The 'gridshell' structures designed by Buro Hoppold reflect this ethos. The feature is constructed from a green oak timber lattice, which is connected to a sweet chestnut base by means of stainless steel bolts and cables. The structure, which creates a most appealing and enclosing mound-like form, represents a bringing together of ancient and traditional practices of working with unseasoned and untreated timber

whilst also incorporating modern technologies, which increase the strength and stability of the design. Sweet chestnut has been specified for the supporting posts because it is extremely durable even when in contact with the ground and does not require the use of timber preservatives, which may be harmful to the environment. Oak and

Above. **Built for long term sustainability, the gridshell at the Earth Centre features the same timeless latticework as has been used since Roman times.**

sweet chestnut are also considered to be native species, available locally and therefore a potentially more sustainable option than imported timber.

The unifying of different materials is also beautifully illustrated in the work of Erik Glemme, who was responsible in the 1940s and 1950s for the development of the Stockholm park system in Sweden. A feature of his design for the Mälarstrand, a linear park running along the shore of Lake Mälaren, was the hop hut. Although the design is perhaps a little old to be considered truly

and specifically the use of timber laminates have enabled designers to build much larger and more ambitious pergola structures as they are no longer restricted to standard timber sizes. Timber laminates are manufactured by glue bonding together smaller sections of wood to create a single beam, which may be capable of spanning many metres. The photograph taken near Barcelona's waterfront illustrates how this technique has been applied to construct a timber laminate bridge. Note the size of the timbers and impressive dimensions of the

The vast timber laminate bridge near Barcelona's waterfront is another fine demonstration of the potential of this new timber technology.

Left. **The two photographs of Erik Glemme's hop huts show a simple idea beautifully realised.**

contemporary, these are nevertheless beautiful structures, which may inspire other more modern interpretations drawing on their unusual form and elegant detailing. Each hop hut consists of a low stone circular wall on to which iron clasps are secured. The clasps hold in place tall slender poles, which are inclined over the central space. The poles provide a simple framework on which hop plants grow, a gentle reference to a Swedish farming tradition of using the flowers in brewing beer. The overall effect is quite magical, in summer the poles and hop plants create an area of dappled shade in which to sit or where children can play. In the Scandinavian winter the repeated structure of circular stone wall and skeletal poles animate the lakeside promenade.

Recent developments in timber technology

entire structure. Although such large timbers may be of little use in the private garden it is possible to adapt this method to create long curved timber beams, which are extremely strong and elegant. The technique has been applied to create entrance pergolas at garden centres. The curved cross-timbers appear very slender, but they are strong enough to support a canopy which will provide shelter in bad weather. It would not be possible to create an equivalent structure from a single piece of timber. Even if a suitably large piece of wood were available there would be tremendous wastage in shaping it to a curve and it would not be strong enough to carry the required loads.

The next examples are taken from the Parc Atlantique, which lies on top of the Paris Montparnasse train station, the terminus for trains to

These two pages feature a variety of contemporary interpretations of pergola-like structures and demonstrate some of the many ways in which modern steel can be used.

Right. The steel structure in the courtyard garden of the Museum of Garden History's garden at the Ark is a lively reinterpretation of Victorian ironwork with eastern overtones.

Left and above. A painted metal tunnel frames the southern edge of the Queen Mother's Garden in Regent's Park. It makes use of the parabolic curve in a modern update of the traditional tunnel arbour. A white rose and purple clematis clamber over the wide welcoming entrance at the angled cross section. The underplanting is a very effective combination of *Alchemilla mollis* with eryngiums.

Above. Dramatic creepers scramble up the walls and along the wires in this very novel use of tensioned wire to roof the walkway round the drum of the Imax cinema in the middle of a roundabout at Waterloo in London.

Right. An elegant stainless steel pergola has here been ingeniously used to disguise the entrance to an underground car park in central Vienna.

the south west coast. These two examples have been included because they illustrate not only how designers can use different materials to create eye-catching features, but perhaps more importantly how the pergola can also be used to embellish the metaphor which underpins the whole design. The park, which was designed by the landscape archi-tects François Brun and Michel Pena in 1992, tells the story of the journey the Parisians would take each summer when they boarded the train and went on holiday to the Atlantic coast. This marine metaphor and the idea of the journey are used to shape and enrich the design in all its details both in construction and planting. The first illustration

Marine metaphors in the Parc Atlantique, Paris, designed by François Brun and Michel Pena in 1992.

The dramatic scuptural promenade created by Enric Mirrales for the Barcelona Olympic games.

shows a tubular stainless steel pergola rising out of the wooden sundeck, which is inclined like the deck of a boat at sea. The pergola is functional in dividing the space and is intended to provide a support on to which vines will grow. Establishing climbing plants on to such smooth metal surfaces can be problematic. Similar features resolve this difficulty by incorporating thin steel cables, next to the post. The second illustration taken from this park is perhaps more explicit and obvious in its form. Produced from pressed stainless steel it creates on a sunny day a shimmering splash of light, which straddles the pathway. Here the designers

exploit the reflective qualities of the material and the flexibility of the thin sheets. Both structures show how different materials enable the designer to explore exciting and unconventional forms.

The final example and definitely the most visually dramatic structure was designed by the Catalan born architect Enric Mirrales as part of the redevelopment of Barcelona in preparation for the Olympic games of 1992. The pergola forms a massive sculptural piece which runs along the central avenue of the Olympic village. In developing the design Mirrales refers to the context in which the structure is placed. This, however, is not the surrounding buildings, for these had not yet been built in this new suburb of Icaria. Instead Mirrales introduces something which links the old cemetery and the profile of Montjuïc mountain where the sporting arenas would be built: 'I wanted the structures to grow as a promenade between these two elements'. It is a massive structure built from tubular steel on to which timber planks are attached. At a functional level the pergola addresses the need to create shade and a more intimate scale in this exposed avenue where underground services constrained the planting of trees. It also has a playful quality, which is revealed in the fragmented shadows, and broken skyline which might echo the experience of washing suspended high above the streetscape which can be seen in the adjacent suburbs.

In its use of specially fabricated tubular steel and in its sheer size this final example would appear to offer little to the garden designer. It is included here not because of its use of individual materials but primarily because of the way in which it brings these materials together in a most striking and challenging form. Each of the examples reviewed, perhaps with the exception of the timber laminate pergola, are individual and unique. They demonstrate how designers have explored and exploited the special qualities of different materials and show how the structure itself can be used to enrich a design in both a playful and perhaps a more meaningful way. For the garden designer and enthusiast it is hoped that these examples will be a source of inspiration which halt the duplication, without question, of what has already been achieved and encourage instead something new and distinctive.

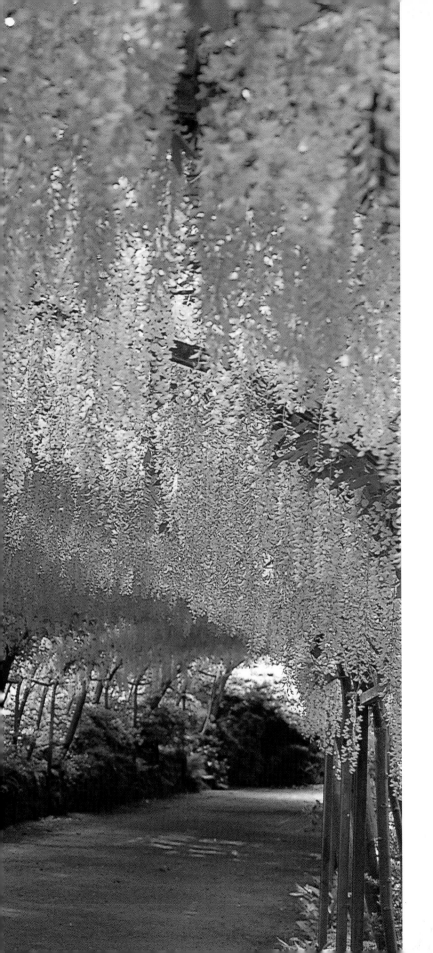

PART TWO

A Garden Tour: Five of the Finest Pergolas

KATHERINE SWIFT

The laburnum tunnel at Bodnant, a simple structure with a spectacular effect. All the trees are pruned hard every January, when much of the old wood is cut out and the new growths tied in. A rolling programme of replacement is practised, with a mixture of old and young trees *in situ* at any one time.

Introduction

Top. Hestercombe (photograph 1950s), designed by Gertrude Jekyll and Edwin Lutyens, 1905.

Centre left. The Hill (photograph 1918), designed by Thomas Mawson, 1905-20.

Centre right. Bodnant (photograph 1920), designed by Henry McLaren, 1914.

Bottom left. West Dean (photograph *c.*1934) designed by Harold Peto, 1911-12.

Bottom right. Great Fosters (photograph 1922), designed by W.H.Romaine-Walker and Gilbert Jenkins, 1918.

The golden age of the pergola was the Edwardian era, that brief charmed interlude between the death of Victoria and the catastrophe of the First World War, when an alliance of landed aristocracy and American money, energised by a newly rich class of industrialists and businessmen, combined to produce that heady social mix of leisure, sensuality and affluence that is typified for us now by the novels of Edith Wharton and Henry James, the paintings of James Tissot and John Singer Sargent, and above all by those countless black and white photographs recording the circuit of lavish country house parties whose presiding spirit was Edward himself – all played out against a backdrop of opulently remodelled and enlarged houses and sumptuous gardens.

The pergola, with its open invitation to stroll and to idle away the hours in scented dalliance, was a potent symbol of that affluence and leisure. The five pergolas surveyed here, all built between 1905 and 1914, with W.H.Romaine-Walker and Gilbert Jenkins's designs for Great Fosters following in 1918, not only exemplify the Edwardian pergola at its best, but also demonstrate the transition from Arts and Crafts Movement to Edwardian classicism, from structures grounded in the English vernacular tradition to those inspired by the imported ideals of the Italian Renaissance. The two styles for a time co-existed, with Jekyll's Hestercombe exemplifying the one and Thomas Mawson's The Hill the other, before the high tide of classicism triumphed, reaching its apotheosis in the work of Harold Peto as exemplified at West Dean. This was a transition that even Lutyens himself, Jekyll's partner in the exquisite realisation of

Hestercombe, was to make. But in lesser hands than Peto's the Italianate style could become coarse, mannered or, as in some of Lutyens's later work, coldly monumental.

By the time that Gertrude Jekyll wrote her *Gardens for Small Country Houses* in 1912, she felt it necessary to devote a whole chapter to the pergola, remarking upon its recent popularity in England: 'twenty years ago it had hardly been thought of. But now… so popular has it become that there is scarcely an example of a modern garden design in which it does not find a place'. The trouble was that many of these pergolas, copied from grander gardens, were badly sited and poorly designed, as Jekyll was quick to point out, and she filled her chapter with examples good and bad for the instruction of her readers.

We can still learn much today about designing, building and planting such structures from a study of the pergola in the hands of master designers such as Harold Peto and Jekyll herself, and from gifted amateurs like Henry McLaren (later Lord Aberconway), who created the lovely sequence of trelliswork pergolas at Bodnant. From Thomas Mawson and his client W.H.Lever (later Lord Leverhulme), we can learn how a pergola can brilliantly resolve the difficulties of a very difficult site. And from the work of Romaine-Walker and Gilbert Jenkins at Great Fosters we can learn how even very simple structures can powerfully contribute to the atmosphere of a garden, by careful siting and inspired planting.

Note: All five pergolas are in gardens which are open to the public. See page 163 for details.

Hestercombe

All pergolas are about the interplay of light and shade, sunshine and shadow, but Hestercombe perhaps above all. Poised on the edge of the Quantocks, looking out over the broad Vale of Taunton towards the Blackdown Hills, this is a garden flooded with light – the two terraces pushing out from the house, the Great Plat beneath, the two flanking water gardens – all drenched in light, but light that is shaped and moulded by architectural detail. The four flights of quadrant steps down into the Great Plat are ripples of alternate light and shade; the recessed slate-lined caverns from which descend the rills on either side are pools of shadow beneath the brilliantly-lit line of the terrace; even the water – standing, flowing, falling, in basins, rills and pools – is alternately shadowy and

deep-set or sparkling with captured light, alternately polished obsidian or molten silver. And the silvery-grey morte slate of Hestercombe, a sedimentary sandstone quarried on site which naturally splits into thin uneven layers, is used all over the garden – in walls, paths, steps and structures of every kind – to give pattern and texture, holding, reflecting, playing with the light.

The pergola is 230 feet (70 metres) long, and forms the whole southern boundary of the formal garden, an airy walkway raised high up above the Plat, joining the two water gardens on either side. It is a place of softly dappled light and shade, intended as a contrast to the broad light of the garden beyond. Within the pergola the patterns and textures multiply. The naturally riven slate

paving slabs (best on a day of sun and showers when their rippled surfaces and uneven edges hold the rain in little puddles and wet gleams) in sunshine are barred with the shadows of the timbers overhead – the heavier beams placed cross-wise, and the stringers running longitudinally, emphasising the receding perspective. At each end, oval *clair voyées* with frames of narrow clustered slivers of slate pierce the walls, allowing green views of the fields beyond, and the morning and evening light to spill on to the flagstones inside. There are 16 square and 24 round pillars, arranged not quite alternately, each with the merest suggestion of base and capital. They are built from the same layered silvery-grey sandstone as the rest of the garden, with the same recessed joints, imitating the effect of dry stone walling. Elsewhere in the garden these crevices provide homes for self-seeded erigeron, white valerian, lavender and santolina, but here the joints are carefully brushed out to maximise the effect of the light, which in the pergola is particularly subtle. This is best appreciated in winter,

or before the canopy of leaves closes, when it will be perceived that the two different sorts of pillars attract and shed light in quite different ways, the square pillars with strongly contrasted light and dark sides, the round ones softer and brighter, so that a rhythm of dark and light pillars alternates all along the pergola walk.

Although the cross beams of the pergola are original, their effect is considerably less massive than intended, since they were cut down to half their depth in 1974. In the process they also lost much of their original canted shape. It is thought that the rotting of the timbers was exacerbated by water collecting in the notches cut for the stringers in the top of each beam. The stringers themselves are now of tannalised softwood, but have the same triangular profile as the originals – a trick to make them appear less heavy from below, perhaps, without sacrificing strength, while also making the whole structure more stable and resistant to wind. That strong winds can blow across the valley was amply demonstrated in January 1995, when five

Previous pages, main picture. Rose 'American Pillar' on the pergola at Hestercombe. Hard pruning is important, not only to prevent the canopy becoming too heavy for the structure, but also to preserve Gertrude Jekyll's intended effect of dappled shade and pools of light.

Previous page. The Great Plat at Hestercombe. The roof line of the pergola breaks at each end to allow unimpeded views from the water terraces along the rills and out into the landscape. This is not felt inside the pergola, where the uprights of the pillars continue in unbroken perspective.

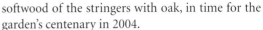

Left. Gertrude Jekyll always
maintained that the cross
beams of pergolas should
rise slightly in the centre to
counteract any tendency to
droop. The original great cross
timbers at Hestercombe shown
in these 1982 photographs
were chosen from naturally
curved timbers.

Below. The importance of the
view back from the stream to
the pergola is underlined by
Miss Jekyll's original planting
plan, which gives details of
border and wall plantings at
the foot of the steeply sloping
south side. These include
Rose 'Natalie Nypels', dwarf
lavenders and *Iris unguicularis*.

pillars collapsed during a storm. The pillars do not have a central core, and the cross beams are attached to the pillars only by their own weight, lodged on a pebble set in the top of the pillar, to allow the different materials to expand and contract naturally. Rebuilding without a core presented some difficulties, eventually solved by suspending a former of the same dimensions above the pillar, and attaching it by strings to the base, the strings then providing guidelines for successive courses of masonry. It is hoped to renew all the timbers, returning the cross beams to their original proportions and replacing the tannalised

softwood of the stringers with oak, in time for the garden's centenary in 2004.

The garden was created by Sir Edwin Lutyens and Gertrude Jekyll between 1904 and 1909. Their client was the Hon. Edward Portman, whose grandfather the 1st Viscount Portman had bought the house in 1873. Viscount Portman had extensively remodelled the house, adding to it the Victorian terrace which still exists on the south front, and a shrubbery on the higher north side between the house and the existing very famous landscape garden designed and laid out by Coplestone Warre Bampfylde between 1750 and 1790. In order to link the shrubbery and landscape garden with his new formal garden, Lutyens built the monumental Daisy Steps, looking down across the west front of the house and out over the garden, to the Vale of Taunton and the Blackdown Hills beyond. Lutyens and Jekyll always preferred to design both house and garden. Here the house was not only preexisting but unsympathetic, a mish-mash of French, Italian and Greek elements faced with hard pink diorite stone. Lutyens's solution was to sidestep the house and the Victorian terrace entirely, leading the eye always out and down, towards the pergola and the view. The formal garden effectively turns its back on the house.

The pergola is crucial to the plan, framing the view, softly delineating the edge of the formal garden, effecting the transition from formal to informal landscape. It is in view right from the start – its roof at first a strong horizontal at the base of the distant prospect as viewed from the top of the Daisy Steps. Then as you descend to the first level of the west water terrace, its position on the edge of the far terrace becomes clear, and you start to see over it, into the valley, like a sort of flowery ha-ha. Nearer still, and you begin to see through the pergola, miniaturised by distance into a rose-festooned balustrade echoing the balustrading which divides the upper and lower water terrace. And finally as you descend by degrees from the water terrace to the sunken floor of the Great Plat, the pergola rises up above you, sheltering and enclosing, and the valley drops away and the wide landscape contracts to a long swelling skyline beneath the beams of the pergola roof, silhouetted now against the sky. The rills whose progress you have followed down the garden discharge at last

into rectangular pools at each end of the pergola, flanked by beds of shrub roses. It is a surprise, on finally reaching it, to find the pergola lower and more intimate than you imagined. It stands on a broad grassy terrace of its own, fronted by a generous border of shrubs and perennials on the garden side, and underplanted with grey-leaved lavenders, phlomis and santolina on the sunny south-facing side. Beyond the pergola is now all meadow: but the garden prospect used to continue with an orchard and lawns leading down to a sinuous stream and waterside path, all planted informally by Miss Jekyll.

Edward Portman died in 1911, and although Mrs Portman survived him by many years, maintenance was an increasing struggle which led ultimately to the break-up of the estate, sold in 1944 to Crown Estates who clear-felled the landscape garden for its timber. The house and formal gardens were let from 1952 to Somerset Fire Brigade, and eventually purchased in 1976 by Somerset County Council. The restoration of the formal gardens began in 1973, by which time there were problems with crumbling stonework and perennial weeds like ground elder and bindweed, and the circulation of water throughout the formal

garden needed a major overhaul. These problems have now been triumphantly overcome. The landscape garden was rescued by a separate trust, which began work in 1995. Happily the gardens were reunited in 1997 and are now jointly managed by the Hestercombe Gardens Project and Somerset County Council.

Miss Jekyll's working plans had been carefully preserved by a succession of head gardeners despite the changes of ownership, and in 1973-75 they formed the basis for the first phase of restoration. But there was tantalisingly little information about the pergola. A careful record was made of the climbers still *in situ* in the pergola in 1973, and these included a number of probably original plantings like *Forsythia suspensa* and the rose 'American Pillar' (1909), together with jasmines, vines and honeysuckles, as well as other unidentified roses and clematis hybrids. Unfortunately during the restoration these were then augmented with anachronistic choices such as the roses 'Aloha' (1949), 'New Dawn' (1930) and 'Francis E. Lester' (1946). Many of the climbers, especially on the south side, had always tended to underperform, as the soil is very light and sandy, and the south-facing side in particular is very hot and exposed to

Above. **A study in light and shade. The wych-elm arbour above the West Rill at Hestercombe echoes the shape of the hemispherical alcove and pool beneath. The recessed joints in the stonework throughout the garden emphasise the uneveness and the layered effect of the stone, enhancing the play of light.**

The views to and from the pergola at Hestercombe are carefully controlled. Here white rambling roses and *Vitis coignetiae* frame the view out through one of the oval *clair voyées* which punctuate each end of the pergola at Hestercombe.

drying winds. As a result, many of the existing roses suffered from blackspot and mildew. But plans are now afoot to take the planting back closer to what Miss Jekyll may have intended, and the opportunity will be taken to choose roses which will perform better in what is rather a difficult situation.

Looking back from the pergola over the Great Plat, with its strong diagonals of turf and stone, the rising tiers of water gardens on either hand

with their vivid linear plantings, the cliff-like face of the retaining wall planted with the same grey-leaved lavenders and santolinas as the Grey Walk above and the pergola walk behind, the whole composition is of a piece – paths, walls, steps, structures, planting. The only jarring note is the house. This garden has everything to do with the landscape around it, the house nothing. It is an irony that such a masterpiece of a garden should surround such a third-rate house.

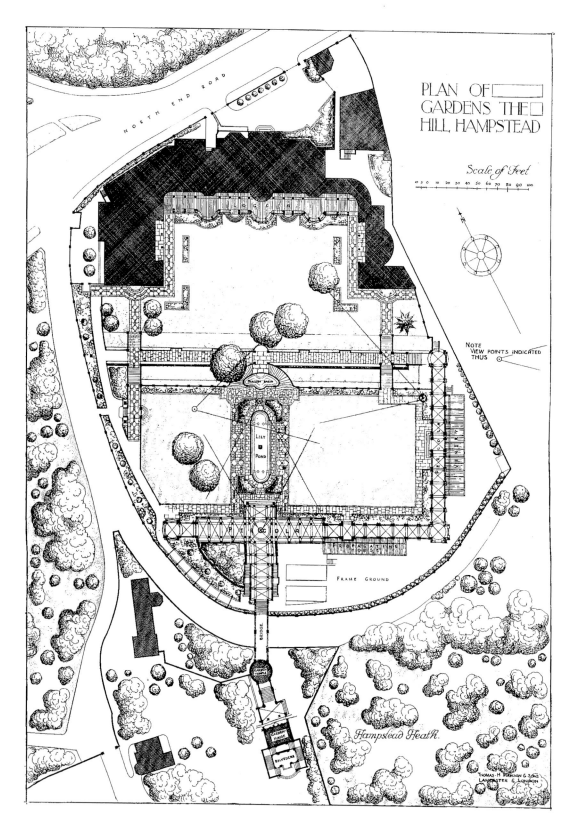

PLAN OF
GARDENS THE
HILL, HAMPSTEAD

Scale of Feet

Left. In Mawson's original conception the whole elaborate structure of the pergola at The Hill revolved upon the pivot of the pergola temple and the facing pool. This plan from his *The Art and Craft of Garden Making* (5th edition 1926) does not not include the final phase of the pergola.

Below. The little domed temple, a brilliant device for disguising an awkward change of direction between the colonnade and the bridge.

The Hill

This remarkable structure with its contradictory signals of exclusivity and openness, its extraordinary scale and brilliantly extempore handling of space, zig-zags around what appears to be a precipice on the edge of the West Heath like some great Indian hill fort, a shimmer of white stone columns above massive red brick arches and buttresses and retaining walls. It changes direction three times, running north, then north-east, then north-west, then north-east again, even before reaching the airy pergola temple on the main axis of the house which seems to be the pergola's natural conclusion. But then the pergola takes another right angle bend north-westwards, running up a flight of steps and over a bridge towards a little round domed temple where it again seems to conclude – only to plunge down and change direction yet again, this time running due west between double rows of columns entwined with the thick knarled trunks of old climbers, the beams overhead with their features blurred by damp and exposure, towards an empty white niche in an apparently blank wall of red brick. And here the pergola finally does seem to end. But negotiate your way around the end wall of the colonnade and across the floor of the summerhouse behind, and suddenly you are outside on the belvedere, high up above the tree tops, with a panoramic view out to the west and the ground falling away all around. It is a magnificent *coup de théâtre*. The sudden feeling of space and light is overwhelming after all the false endings and the claustrophobia of the colonnade.

It is worth the effort to traverse the pergola in this direction if you can, starting from the south via the small gate which gives directly on to the Heath just off North End Way beyond West Heath Brow. The main public access from the north, via Inverforth Close, winds through shrubs and trees to the foot of the steps leading up to the belvedere.

Approached from this direction, the whole experience of the pergola can only be a diminuendo, tailing off to the south instead of the gradual crescendo which culminates in the crashing final chord of that western view.

Stylistically, too, the pergola falls into three sections which build towards a crescendo at the western end. The long zig-zag of the southern pergola is the simplest, with its lighter construction of single rows of paired two-thirds-height concrete Doric columns carried on stone balustrades, with straight oak beams running across overhead, and a roof line punctuated by the southern belvedere and the southern summerhouse, together with various other arched structures marking each change of direction. Then comes the wider and more elaborate cruciform central pergola on the axis of the house, with spaciously-set pairs of double and single full-height Doric columns of Portland stone, centred on the taller space of the pergola temple with its open tented roof of upcurved oak beams. And finally, there is the intricately composed western colonnade, almost 100 metres (330 feet) long – a forest of two double rows of closely spaced double and single full-height Portland stone Doric columns running from the small domed temple above the bridge to the western summerhouse and belvedere, with massed short pergola beams carried between adjacent pairs of beams within the double rows, leaving a narrow strip of sky overhead.

In all, the pergola is some 245 metres (800 feet) long. The manipulation of space is masterly. The colonnade is the longest continuous length, and the tug of the perspective is deliberately emphasised by the treatment of the floor. Elsewhere in the pergola the floors are of Portland stone slabs, with the perspective gently reinforced by longer slabs laid longitudinally along each side. But here a narrow strip of red brick, banded by

Above. The working parts of the garden were originally screened from view by the base of the pergola. They are now planted as ornamental gardens in their own right.

Lower left. The south-west corner of the pergola was completely rebuilt following damage in the storms of 1987 and 1990. With few if any detailed records of its construction to go on, remaining fragments were used as patterns to supply missing parts, together with contemporary photographs, plans and descriptions.

Lower right. The Summer Pavilion now overlooks a new garden on the original site of the vinery.

Above. Some elements of earlier planting survive here, sheltered from the north by solid south-facing walls. The forest of columns, the solid walls and the heavy planting induce a feeling of mild claustrophobia which only serves to heighten the experience of the belvedere itself. The whole point of the colonnade is to look along the length of it, to enjoy the narrowed perspective of floor and column invaded by the trailing tendrils of the climbers, with that deceptively blank wall at one end and the steps leading up to the little domed temple at the other.

Right. The reconstructed timber roof of the pergola temple at The Hill. Both green and air-dried oak was used in the new timber superstructure of the pergola to minimise distortion, and a new lead lining was placed between the new timbers and the stonework to protect the stone from acid decay.

courses of white stone and anchored by a circular white stone motif in the floor at each end, runs the entire length of the colonnade. The little temple itself with its solid walls and raised position is a brilliant disguise for an awkward 'elbow', occasioned by the pergola's change of direction at that point.

The central pergola consists of balancing north and south arms each terminating in arched structures, a western arm connecting with the bridge, and a short stub of an eastern arm framing the formal lily pond and double flight of curving steps up to the house. This is the centre of the whole pergola, the pivot upon which the whole elaborate structure turns – a fact emphasised by the dramatic up-thrust of the roof timbers above the crossing. This is also the point where pergola, house and garden interconnect. The house, framed in the central opening of the pergola, is Neo-Georgian in style, of red brick with white details, very long and very low. Its entire west front, crowning the top of the slope facing the pergola, is spanned by a loggia of white Portland stone Doric columns, echoed in size, style and orientation by the pergola at its foot.

If the colonnade discourages views out, the southern arm of the pergola at the opposite end seems to invite them. The balustrading here echoes the balustrade across the front of the house and at the top of the steps in the formal garden, and it invites you to lean over and look out and through and down, to a surprisingly varied series of scenes – on one side to manicured grass, formal water and gently rising ground to the house, on the other side into the tree tops and the wilder landscape of the Heath, or diagonally to the little domed temple and a series of compositions of startling Piranesi-like complexity.

The pergola was built by the landscape architect Thomas Mawson for W.H. Lever, subsequently Lord Leverhulme, in three phases between *circa* 1905-6, 1911-14 and 1917-1920. This reflects Lever's piecemeal acquisition of the site, and in turn is reflected by the three stylistic divisions still seen today. The first phase of construction was the central cruciform pergola and the narrower L-shape of the southern pergola, running south and east. Together they enclosed the property known as The Hill, which Lever had bought in

1904. Lever had gardens elsewhere, at Thornton Manor in Cheshire and at 'The Bungalow' (Roynton Cottage) near Rivington in Lancashire – at both of which Mawson was also employed – and all three gardens shared a common function: they had to be able to accommodate the large garden parties and fêtes which Lever was in the habit of throwing for employees, good causes and his wide circle of acquaintances. The site at The Hill posed special problems, however, because the ground sloped steeply down to Hampstead Heath, from where the garden was totally overlooked. The contemporaneous construction of the Hampstead extension of the London Underground system offered an ingenious solution. In return for a modest fee, Lever contracted to dispose of the spoil excavated from the tunnels via the nearby Golders Green station, thus raising the ground level at The Hill by 7-10 metres (20-30 feet). The

The southern pergola 'closely screened' by climbers on trellis as photographed in 1918. Mawson's own planting plans seem to have vanished, but the 1912 issue of the *Gardeners' Chronicle* mentions pyrus, japonica, jasmines, various clematis hybrids, Rose 'Crimson Rambler' and wisteria.

new garden was terraced, carefully retaining the mature trees, and laid to lawn, with a pergola erected on top of the new retaining walls to shield Lever and his guests from the gaze of people passing on the Heath. The central pergola at this point in time contained a conservatory on the western arm and an elliptical seating bay.

In 1911 Lever purchased neighbouring Heath Lodge to the north west, demolished the house, and began to lay out a garden. The problem now was how to integrate the new piece of ground with the existing garden, not least because the two properties were at an angle to one another, and were separated by a public right of way. The equally ingenious solution here was to demolish the conservatory, throw a bridge over the right of way, and continue the pergola out towards the west, disguising the awkward change of direction by means of the little domed temple, and guaranteeing the privacy of the new garden by the closely spaced pillars and solid south-facing walls of the colonnade along the new boundary.

The third and final phase of construction was delayed until after the First World War, by which time Lever (now Lord Leverhulme) had already bought Cedar Lawn, the adjoining property to the south. The house again had already been demolished, and the problem was once more to link the two gardens and to give the new garden more privacy from passers-by on the Heath. An additional 115 metres (380 feet) were added to the original L-shape of the southern pergola, incorporating a new summerhouse and a southern belvedere.

After Lord Leverhulme's death in 1925, The Hill and its pergola experienced a long slow decline. By 1960, the garden was in considerable disrepair when the Heath Lodge grounds, including the colonnade, were separated from the rest of the garden and bought by the London County Council, who restored them and opened them to the public in 1963. The remainder of the pergola, comprising the central and southern sections, was separated from the house in 1985 and ownership transferred first to the Greater London Council and subsequently to the Corporation of London.

Already weakened by unchecked growth of the climbers, rotting and twisting of wooden beams which had been used green, acid decay to the capitals and bases of the stonework where they had come into contact with the oak timbers, and subsidence of the retaining walls which had been built upon made-up ground, these sections suffered further damage and in places total collapse as a result of the storms of 1987 and 1990.

During the comprehensive programme of rebuilding and restoration which followed, the opportunity was taken to adapt the pergola to its new situation. Without sacrificing the important visual links between the pergola and garden, the house had to be made secure and an attempt made to provide stronger links between the pergola and the Heath. The trelliswork was renewed on the garden side, with steel replacing the original wooden construction, and the various points of access between pergola and garden closed with new trelliswork borrowed from other designs by Mawson. The summerhouse on the pergola's southern extension was rotated through 180 degrees, so that the viewing platform faced the Heath and the solid wall faced the garden. And the areas outside the pergola, which were the site of the 'garden offices' – the west-facing area enclosed between the south and west arms of the central pergola where the frames and propagating house used to be, and the favoured south-facing area below the southern pergola which used to house the vinery (all intended to be invisible from the house and formal garden) – were developed as ornamental gardens in their own right.

Despite its extravagant scale and grandiloquent gestures, the pergola at The Hill still has much to say to us today, not least in the handling of a difficult site and in its brilliant manipulation of space. And although it is no longer possible to view the pergola from the house and garden which it was designed to enclose, it is still possible in one important respect to experience the pergola as Lord Leverhulme and his guests originally did, by walking westward from the house along that magnificent colonnade and seeing that final view out over London for the first time.

Bodnant

Sometimes it is the planting of a pergola which occupies centre-stage, the structure itself going almost unnoticed. But even the simplest of structures may conceal hidden subtleties. The structure of the laburnum tunnel at Bodnant could hardly be more simple, consisting of T-section lengths of curving iron bolted together and painted light green, with plain wooden laths tied together in between as stringers. Despite its economy of means, there is great elegance and artistry here – in the S-bend of the smooth olive-green tree trunks, as they lean into the tunnel, sway-backed; in the wide shallow pitch of the roof, low enough to dangle the flowers almost within reach of your nose; and in the generous width of the path, splashed with sunlight and a scattering of fallen blossoms – but above all in the curve of the whole structure, its end disappearing out of sight as it follows the wall and the road above, disguising the tunnel's length and its ultimate goal. It is not only that wonderful colour which so excites the eye, it is the dynamism of the shape. Being inside the laburnum tunnel in flower is like being inside a curving hollow surf-wave on the point of crashing on to the shore, all sparkling sunshine and spray (page 74).

The laburnum tunnel (known at Bodnant as the laburnum arch and at various times in the past as the laburnum arbour or the laburnum pergola) was planted sometime between 1875 and 1888 by the present Lord Aberconway's great-grandfather, Henry Pochin. During its 120-odd years of existence it has undergone a number of changes, refining both planting and proportions. The original planting, probably of the common European *Laburnum anagyroïdes* (smaller than the British native *Laburnum alpinum*, and with shorter racemes but larger flowers), was gradually replaced after 1928 by the new hybrid between the two species, *Laburnum* x *watereri* 'Vossii', which has the longer racemes of *Laburnum alpinum* and the larger flowers of *Laburnum anagyroïdes*. The use of the new hybrid, which is much more free-flowering than either of its parents, would have lowered the flowering canopy by as much as 25 centimetres (9 or 10 inches). The width of the path has changed too: inside the tunnel on both sides were scallop-topped yew hedges, clothing the bases of arches and trees almost to head height, making the path much narrower and darker than it is today. And even the colour scheme has not always been quite as we see it now: for a time the laburnum was interplanted with wisteria, probably added in the late 1920s when it was so fashionable.

Both hedges and wisteria were removed sometime after 1931, and the banks on either side were planted as we see them today with pink and white azaleas which flower at the same time as the laburnum, making the path at once wider and brighter, and the whole tunnel lighter in mood. This seems to have been part of a general brightening of the palette in the garden at Bodnant during the 1930s and 1940s, as the great collection of rhododendrons and magnolias (favoured by Bodnant's acid soil and high rainfall and planted extensively from 1910 onwards) gradually matured.

Bodnant is situated on the brink of the deep wooded gorge of the River Hiraethlyn, looking across to the peaks of Snowdonia on the skyline opposite. That view, and the topography of the gorge below, were to dictate the whole future development of the garden. When Henry Pochin bought Bodnant in 1874, it was a plain white square house of the early 1790s, set amid green slopes. His twin passions were the house – which he encased in local blue-grey stone with buff-coloured Talacre dressings, and embellished with double-height bow windows, conservatory and Tudor gables (tactfully veiled by the next generation with *Pyracantha coccinea* 'Lalandei') – and the remarkable collection of exotic conifers which he planted all along the slopes of the river, in what

Previous pages, main picture. **The coolly elegant North pergola at Bodnant supports magnificent specimens of white wisteria and pale grey blue *Clematis* x *jouiniana*. Beyond it, in complete contrast, is a small garden of hot colours and exotic planting, including yuccas, phormiums, cordylines, palm trees and lilies.**

Previous page. **The laburnum tunnel at Bodant, *c.*1930, before the laburnums were replaced by the more floriferous *Laburnum* x *watereri* 'Vossii'. The gloomy effect of the yew hedges is in striking contrast to the brilliance of the more recent plantings of azaleas.**

Below. **The Canal Terrace, photographed by *Country Life* in 1920, with the curving pergola behind soon after construction. The buttresses, parapets and retaining wall are still only partially clothed with climbers.**

became known as The Dell. The great sequence of five Italianate terraces carved out of the precipitous slope below the house was the creation of Mr Pochin's grandson, Henry McLaren, later 2nd Lord Aberconway. He was entrusted by his mother Laura (who had inherited Bodnant in 1895 on her father's death) with the care and development of the gardens from about 1901 onwards. By 1903 he had already conceived the idea for the terraces, and by 1905 the first three had been constructed. The two lower terraces were added, after a break of some years, immediately before the 1914-18 war. The scheme was finally completed in 1939 with the re-erection of the Pin Mill on the bottom and last terrace (the Canal Terrace).

Occupying all the high retaining wall between the third and fourth terraces and providing the backdrop to the fourth and fifth, is a structure as flamboyantly ornamental in construction as the laburnum arch is functional: the rose pergola. You come upon it almost unexpectedly. As you descend

the great series of terraces, each of the formal terraced gardens folds out one below the other like pages from a pop-up book, each one concealing the delights of the next until the last minute: first the Upper Rose Terrace, then the Croquet Terrace, then the Lily Terrace, rippling towards the view in a lovely series of concentric curves. And then as you begin the descent from the Lily Terrace towards the Lower Rose Terrace, the pergola opens out under your feet. Like the laburnum arch, it curves, hugging the retaining wall below you. But here the architecture is everything. It is made of wooden trellis, stained blue-grey, with square openwork pillars, cross beams and architrave all constructed from the same diamond-pattern trellis, the pillars with solid wooden bases and capitals, the roofline decorated with elegant wooden urns. It is a virtuoso display of pattern and texture, its playfulness contrasting with the serenity of the Lily Terrace above, and the formality of the Canal Terrace below. The pergola is of two storeys, the

lower swelling out in front of the upper. The upper pergola is narrower, lower in height, but longer, the ends disappearing out of view. Was this curving Italianate pergola Henry McLaren's homage to his grandfather's laburnum arch?

The combined height of the two storeys and the curving steps which enclose them is six metres (20 feet), and every surface is festooned with ramblers and scramblers of every kind – trained over the parapet walls of the steps, cascading down from the terrace above, entwined in the trellis of the pergola itself – while in the bays against the descending walls and in the shelter beneath the pergola nestle tender wall-trained shrubs such as *Carpenteria californica*, *Ceanothus*, *Crinodendrons*, *Drimys winteri*, *Leptospermums* and tender rhododendrons and camellias. Although close to the sea, the climate here is not especially mild (thousands of rhododendrons, for example, were lost in the winter of 1981-2), and the west-facing pergola with its deep buttresses provides a useful microclimate.

The pergola itself is quite lightly covered, retaining a strong architectural presence against the backdrop of the wall shrubs' glossy evergreen foliage. The colour scheme is white, cream, yellow and soft blue – exquisitely simple – carried through in flowers, woodwork and stone. There are cream and yellow roses, such as 'Easlea's Golden Rambler' and 'Climbing Lady Hillingdon', and lavender blue *Solanum crispum* 'Glasnevin' with its rich yellow centres; two magnificent specimens of the lovely deep cream rambler 'Gardenia' on either side of the central opening of the lower pergola, flanked by matching specimens of wall-trained *Magnolia grandiflora* 'Goliath' with its intensely fragrant white flowers; and an underplanting of *Libertia grandiflora*, with spiky rush-like leaves and tall stiff stems of tiny white flowers in billowing masses throughout the pergola – all set off against the blue of the trellis, the soft yellow of the York stone paths and parapets, and the grey-blue of the walls.

Down on the terrace below are two more trelliswork pergolas at right angles to the retaining wall, enclosing the rose parterre. Unlike the curving pergola, these two structures are free-standing, and are much more exposed to the south-westerly gales which can sweep the valley. The planting on the North pergola includes an ancient white wisteria, its trunk as thick as your waist, with

Left. The blue stained wooden trelliswork of the central curving pergola at Bodnant is perfectly complemented by the soft tones of the blue and yellow planting. Here *Ceanothus* 'Cascade' is partnered with Rose 'Climbing Lady Hillingdon'.

Shade-loving white *Libertia grandiflora*, here in the South pergola, grows in great abundance at Bodnant.

pearly late-flowering *Clematis* x *jouiniana* at the opposite end. Much of the planting of the South pergola is relatively young, having been recently renewed after this pergola collapsed in the storm of Christmas 1997. Each pillar is now strengthened by galvanised steel box-section reinforcements inside the wooden base.

Pergolas are costly to maintain – their structures subject to decay and collapse, their planting in need of regular renewal and dedicated atten-

tion, and it is due in very large measure to the continuity of ownership and staffing at Bodnant that both the laburnum arch and the pergolas have continued in such excellent health, watched over by Henry McLaren and his son Charles (3rd Lord Aberconway), spanning between them a century of gardening at Bodnant, and by three generations of the Puddle family, as head gardeners and now managers in unbroken succession from 1920 to the present day.

Peto's pergola at West Dean is the embodiment of Edwardian opulence, heavy with scent, redolent of the romance of warmer climes. To stroll down the pergola and gaze at the lily tank, descending at last into the rose parterre, must have been the high point of many a summer house party.

West Dean

Gertrude Jekyll always maintained that a pergola should have somewhere to go. The pergola at West Dean contradicts this rule, seeming to be gloriously unconnected with the rest of the garden, a splendid irrelevance. Standing in isolation in the middle of the surrounding lawns, it assumes almost temple-like status. Indeed, the quality of the stonework is in certain respects so fine as to suggest that the columns might well have been rescued from a real temple by some nineteenth-century adventurer. The pergola was designed by Harold Peto, gentleman-architect turned garden designer and connoisseur, whose own garden at Iford Manor near Bath was designed expressly as a repository for his collection of Greek and Roman antiquities.

Peto's clients at West Dean were Mr and Mrs William James, wealthy socialites who entertained in sumptuous style, their guests frequently including Edward VII and his entourage. William James had purchased the house in 1891, and immediately called in the architectural partnership of Harold Peto and Ernest George to modernise and enlarge it. The partnership of Peto and George was dissolved in 1892, with George permitted to use Peto's name until 1895, and Peto giving an undertaking not to practise as an architect in Britain for fifteen years, concentrating instead on his architectural practice on the French Riviera, and on designing gardens. These included a number of important commissions in France, Ireland and England, including West Dean. Peto continued to work at West Dean intermittently throughout the James's period of ownership, writing in 1911 that working at West Dean 'has always been to me a very great pleasure, you and Mrs. Willie are so very appreciative and kind that one feels one wants you to have things Extra nice!'

Peto's French gardens include several exquisite examples of classical pergolas, and at West Dean he used all his accumulated skill to create a pergola of perfect proportions, details and layout. It was designed in August 1911 and built the following winter. The stone columns are tall and slender, with the slight entasis or swelling of their Doric models (see page 113). Each is set singly on a low plinth, widely spaced from its fellows, with a very light superstructure overhead, carried on a square concave-sided slab (the abacus) above each column. Approached from the lawn below, the tapered effect of the columns and their height is accentuated still further, and the whole effect is of lightness and delicacy.

According to his letters, Peto had submitted two designs for the pergola, 'one more classic in detail and the other more Tudor,...the latter more in accord with the house perhaps'. The Tudor scheme had octagonal columns and a plinth made from alternate blocks of dressed flint and stone, arranged chessboard-fashion, as in the house and surrounding walls – 'a charming treatment of flint in Tudor times, much used in Wiltshire'. It seems that the final design for the pergola incorporated elements from both schemes, as the classical pergola we see today stands upon the Tudor-style plinth of flint and stone. Peto's drawings for the pergola seem to be no longer extant and, following substantial storm damage in January 1990, some elements of the pergola's superstructure had to be reconstructed on the basis of surviving photographs, which may or may not accurately reflect the details of Peto's originals.

Apart from freak storms such as those of January 1990 and October 1987, the West Dean estate has a mild climate, being close to the English Channel and sheltered by the South Downs. The garden itself, however, is in a frost pocket. The site chosen for the pergola was on the warmer south-facing slope above the house, but its position there is enigmatic, half way up the lawn, at a slight angle

Left. The garden house at the west end of the pergola at West Dean. Since 1964 West Dean has been owned by the Edward James Foundation, an educational charitable trust, and the window panes of the garden house were etched in 1981 with scenes depicting the different crafts now studied here.

Top right. Following storm damage in 1990, the whole pergola at West Dean was replanted and borders were added across the front of the pergola to anchor it more firmly in its landscape (contrast the photograph on page 76 of Edward James in front of the pergola in 1934).

William James, whose substantial fortune derived in part from the American metals and mining firm Phelps Dodge & Co. He died in 1912.

The interior of the pergola at West Dean showing the lily tank and loggia (c.1920). The original planting was quite light in effect, with climbers trained straight up the columns, in marked contrast to the effect of today's luxuriant planting.

athwart the hillside, apparently leading nowhere, with no formal relation to either house or view. From Peto's letters, it appears that he too acknowledged that the pergola lacked a *raison d'être* – a problem he attempted to solve by adding a 'Garden House' to the design at the western end and proposing to rearrange the existing rose garden (*in situ* by 1898) to supply a suitable terminus at the pergola's eastern end.

The pergola extends from the garden house, with its Tudor details of flint and stone and its domed stone roof, across the lawn in a single line broken by two openings which divide the pergola into three roughly equal thirds. The first opening, marked by an overthrow of a single pair of simple curved wooden beams crossing overhead, is reached by steps up from the lawn through double columns on either side, leading to the site of the former tennis ground on the lawn above. The second and more important opening of the two is marked by a broad flight of steps of double width, leading up from the lawn via a portico – five columns wide – to a loggia which encloses the central portion of the pergola. The line of the pergola continues unbroken through the loggia, the inner columns enclosing a narrow rectangular sunken tank two column-spaces long, the position of which is marked overhead by two further pairs of

curved wooden beams. These wooden 'domes', echoing the dome of the garden house, are part of the 1990 reconstruction work. Now comes the last and shortest section of the pergola, to the east of the loggia, where the pergola ends without ceremony and drops down a flight of steps to the site of the rose garden. This was subsequently laid out as a sunken garden, and later altered again by William's son Edward in the 1930s.

It is evident that it was Peto's plan that the pergola should end in the rose garden, and yet it feels oddly inconclusive and truncated. The pergola is about 90 metres long (about 330 feet), and in his letters Peto acknowledges that 'such a length of pergola' needs some 'delightful interlude' like the tank and its enclosing loggia, to be viewed 'either when walking along the pergola, or looked at from outside'. But the tank is hardly an 'interlude', occurring less than a third of the way along the pergola. Was the pergola intended to be longer? – long enough perhaps to accommodate another domed and columned opening giving access to the rose garden, matching the one giving on to the tennis ground? – long enough even to

reach across the rose garden and as far as the main drive? What exactly was involved when Peto speaks of 'rearranging' the rose garden? William James died in 1912, the year the pergola was built. Had he lived, these problems might have been resolved. He might even have gone on to commission other formal gardens from Peto to complement the pergola. But as it is, the contradictions in the design and siting remain, and the pergola stands, rather stranded, in open lawns dotted with trees and shrubberies, survivals of island beds laid out earlier in the nineteenth century.

Following the collapse of the pergola and its subsequent reconstruction after the storm of January 1990, the pergola was completely replantd by the garden supervisor Sarah Wain. The new planting is an object lesson in how to select and train climbing plants for a pergola. Each pillar is planted with a pair of complementary climbers – rambling roses with late-flowering clematis, clematis with vines, summer jasmine with earlier-flowering clematis – to prolong the flowering period. Honeysuckles and *Trachelospermum asiaticum* were added for their scent and foliage. Colours

Roses 'Crimson Shower', 'Violette' and 'Sanders White' with Clematis 'Venosa Violacea' above the lily tank in the pergola at West Dean. Peto's pergolas were noted for their fine architectural detail.

are rich purples and crimson, shading to paler pinks and white. No two pillars are planted with the same combination, except in the loggia, drawing the eye to the centrepiece of the whole design, with the pillars of the portico planted with the rose 'Sanders White' and *Wisteria floribunda* 'Macrobotrys', enclosing paired pillars of the white clematis 'Marie Boisselot' with white *Jasminum officinale*, and the deep blue-purple rose 'Violette' with clematis 'Venosa Violacea' around the lily pond inside. The planting at the base of the columns, within the pergola, is designed to give interest earlier in the year, consisting of bulbs, primulas and ferns, all lush and green in the shade of the climbers (page 132), whereas the sunny borders outside are used to carry the interest on into the late summer and autumn.

William James was succeeded in 1912 by his five-year-old son Edward, his only son. Only months previously on 5 January 1912 Edward and his four older sisters had marched in procession to the pergola where his mother's diary recalls, 'Edward laid foundation stone of pergola, he was too sweet'. In adult life Edward became a life-long Surrealist, the friend and patron of Magritte and Dali. He was briefly married to the dancer Tilly Losch, a trail of whose bare wet footprints he had had woven into the carpet of the spiral staircase, with matching muddy pawprints of his dog woven into the stair carpet in the hall. Although he lived mainly abroad after the failure of his marriage, he did make some additions to the garden, including the Dragon's Grave (with its mock-serious 'Grave Warning'), made from spoil excavated during the construction of a plunge pool in the sunken garden on the site of the former rose garden. And in 1974 in a typically surrealist gesture – at once poignant and ironic – he commissioned the sculptor Ralph Burton to encase the stumps of two dead beech trees in the spring garden in glass fibre and resin. In the same year the Surrealist Ivan Hicks, who went on to create notable gardens elsewhere, was engaged as head gardener. James died in 1984, having spent 25 years creating a surrealist fantasy of pagodas, temples and fountains on the steep mountain slopes of a Mexican rain forest. It would have been fun to see what he might have done with the idea of a pergola in this quintessentially English setting.

The stems of the climbers at West Dean art trained in criss-cross fashion to ensure that the columns are clothed with flowers and foliage right down to the ground. Each year a proportion of the old stems are cut out and new replacement stems are tied in.

Great Fosters

Like the archetypal English country house which gives the impression of having been continually altered and added to over the centuries and seems to wear its architectural history on its sleeve, the garden at Great Fosters appears to reflect a long history of garden-making by many generations of owners. The medieval moat, the Jacobean parterre, the avenue of venerable limes, the Reptonian rose garden with its beds and surrounding arcade of roses, the Edwardian pergola, the little wisteria-draped bridge with its suggestion of willow-pattern *japonaiserie*, the two Italianate *giardini segreti*, all conjure up images of succeeding periods of English lives lived out in this same spot. Most of this is illusion, of course – pastiche on the part of a clever twentieth-century garden designer – but there is an underlying stratum of truth.

The brief given by the Hon. Gerald Samuel Montagu to W.H.Romaine-Walker and his partner Gilbert Jenkins was 'to recreate the old-world charm of the place'. The core of the house dates from the mid-sixteenth century, but was considerably enlarged in the first decade of the seventeenth. Both phases of building are predated by the moat, which would seem to indicate a manor house on the site from medieval times. The complex was substantially enlarged again in 1635, but during the eighteenth century fell on hard times and was run as a private lunatic asylum. It was extensively restored and remodelled by Baron Colonel Halkett in the middle of the nineteenth century, before falling into neglect once again at the beginning of the twentieth, from which it was rescued in 1918 by Gerald Montagu. Montagu then set about restoring and remodelling it yet again, with Romaine-Walker being responsible for the house and the broad outline of the garden, and Jenkins probably responsible for the detail of the garden and its planting.

Romaine-Walker's design builds on the sur-viving garden and landscape features, taking as its point of departure the U-shaped moat. Almost square (238 metres long by 220 across, 260 x 240 yards), the moat fits the original east front of the house like an apron stage, enclosing a sunken area accessed from a long paved terrace walk across the house. Here he laid out his Jacobean parterre of yew topiary with four square box-edged *parterres de compartiment* and two crossing paths, centred on the old sundial. The longer of the two paths, running outwards from the house, is on the axis of the old entrance drive to the west front of the house, the line of which Romaine Walker continued through the house and parterre and across the moat in a double avenue of lime trees to the south east. The sunken parterre is reflected on the other (south-west) side of the moat by an enclosed area not much less in size, and of similar proportions, where Jenkins laid out his sunken rose garden and the two secret gardens. They are connected to the parterre by the little Japanese bridge, which carries a continuation of the crossing path in the parterre over the moat and through the rose garden; in former times the path was prolonged out beyond the rose garden and across the walled kitchen garden, where it was covered by a tunnel of arched cordon fuit trees. Two very different garden areas are thus welded together by geometry, each revolving around the same axis, but separated by the south-west arm of the moat, and screened one from the other by the long pergola.

The lynchpin of the design is the little Japanese bridge, connecting the dark geometry of the parterre with the romance of the rose garden, its steep humped shape emphasising the passage from one world to another, from the crisp topiary shapes of the one to the swooning roses and scented air of the other. The transition is made all the more dramatic by the bridge itself being enclosed, a secret place in its own right. A stub of

103

Previous page. The formal parterre of yew and box at Great Fosters, looking towards the Japanese bridge and pergola. Both English Heritage and the Surrey Gardens Trust have given grants towards the restoration of the gardens.

Above left. An archive aerial shot of the garden at Great Fosters. Apart from the truncation of the double avenue of limes by the building of the M25 motorway in 1971, the garden has been preserved virtually intact.

Below left. The rose garden at Great Fosters in 1922, showing the original planting, with standard roses lining the grass walk, densely planted bedding roses, and climbing roses clothing the arches right down to the ground.

Right. A glimpse through the pergola at Great Fosters to the wisteria-draped Japanese bridge. Beneath the pergola, on the side facing the moat, the original rock work by Gomer Waterer is interspersed with lush plantings of ferns, hardy geraniums and hellebores.

the pergola reaches out at right angles to embrace the bridge, which is festooned with wisteria – in spring a shimmer of silver-green leaves, in summer a scented tunnel of flower, silvery mauve against the silver-grey of the weathered oak timbers. And in autumn a curtain of pale gold leaves, vivid against the rain-darkened wood of the bridge, trailing down on either side towards the moat, where black swans with red beaks peck the hump-backed curve of the bridge reflected in the dark water. It is a stroke of genius.

The shape and the planting of the bridge, whilst beckoning you on, also conspire to obscure your destination – the opening to the rose garden beyond – which, when it comes, is almost a surprise. A circular arcade of 24 tall rose arches surrounds low beds of roses which themselves encircle a central circular pond. The rose garden is said to have been inspired by a design for Moreton Paddox in Warwickshire by Edward White, Romaine-Walker's collaborator on the gardens there, but it is pure Ashridge and Humphry Repton in conception, right down to the trellis-work bases of the rose arches (see page 52). Jenkins's clever innovation was to sink the middle of the garden, making two concentric sets of rose beds, the outer eight on an inclined plane, and the inner four enclosing the circular lily pool, which is sunk to its brim in the centre of the garden. Eight flights of stone steps divide the slope, which is crowned with the circular rose arcade, looking all the more elegantly attenuated with the ground falling away at its feet. The round of the arcade is enclosed by straight-sided yew hedges on three sides, within which runs a square colonnade of roses – in part a continuation of the pergola and in part a run of single columns linked by running beams with the remaining side supplied by the pergola itself. The relative heights and weights are interesting: the arches, standing on the brim of the sunken portion of the garden, light and delicate, are tallest at about 3.4 metres (11 feet) the square-topped colonnade around it, solid and heavier in construction, is lower at about 2.75 metres (9 feet); and the perimeter yew hedge, darkest and heaviest, is lowest at about 2.3 metres (7½ feet).

The pergola was originally conceived as the backbone of Romaine-Walker's design, carrying the main walkway out into the grounds beyond the formal gardens, but its importance gradually dwindled to little more than a decorative feature when in the early 1930s it was bypassed by a second bridge built across the moat on the main axis from the house. In 1929 Great Fosters had been sold to Harold Sutcliffe, who had remodelled it and opened it as a hotel. The new bridge was to provide a link to the newly constructed swimming pool, hard tennis courts and archery ground. With its proximity to Ascot and the Shepperton Film Studios, Great Fosters became the most fashionable hotel in England during the 1930s, patronised by film stars, debutantes and royalty. It even featured in a Noel Coward play. At the famous annual Great Fosters Ascot Week ball, revellers were encouraged after dining to take midnight archery lessons or a flood-lit dip in the swimming pool. The second bridge has recently been demolished, returning some of the *raison d'être* to the pergola, though at present the outer grounds are considerably less visited than during the heyday of the hotel. However, the acquisition in the year 2000 of an additional 34 acres of surrounding land to be developed as oak woodland and nature reserve may well reverse the trend and restore the pergola's original function. The pergola is planted with a mixture of rambling roses and the evergreen *Clematis armandii*.

In construction the wooden structures of the rose garden and the pergola are quite simple – the

pergola and colonnade uprights being made of green oak with square-section cross beams and stringers of much the same weight, and the arches of single spans of iron on post and trellis bases. The brilliance is all in the placing and the juxtaposition. The structures were partly damaged by the storms of 1987 and 1990. The garden had in general been well maintained, although by 1990 much of the original planting had either disappeared, or was in urgent need of replanting or re-shaping. Only the bridge had been unsympathetically restored, its wooden legs supported in the 1950s with clumsy brick footings. These have now been removed and since 1991 the garden and all its structures have been comprehensively restored and replanted under the supervision of the landscape architect Kim Wilkie.

Great Fosters is a highly theatrical garden, of undeniable charm. But as Anthony Blanche said in *Brideshead Revisited*, 'Charm is the great English blight . . . It kills love; it kills art; I greatly fear, my dear Charles, it has killed you'. In part, the garden at Great Fosters was the expression of a longing to put back the clock and to forget the horrors of the recent war in a celebration of the past – an exercise in which Great Fosters's subsequent reinvention as a setting for debutante balls and high society debauches during the Depression years can be seen as a perpetuation. The irony is that in the process Romaine-Walker himself was submerged by the same tide of willed oblivion. Too clever by half, Romaine-Walker could serve up mock-Tudor or Louis Quatorze with equal conviction, with the result that no one now remembers him at all. He is dismissed as a pasticheur, expunged from the garden history books. But Great Fosters, in its romantic planting and formal design, its grand plan but intimate scale, in its use of small, hedged enclosures, each self-sufficient but linked into a whole, belongs in its own way to the same tradition as much grander gardens like Hidcote, prefiguring even Sissinghurst itself.

The Japanese bridge over the moat at Great Fosters links the formal parterre with the romantic rose garden. The air of *japonaiserie* around the moat is further enhanced by a tall weeping willow laced with white wisteria, trailing its tendrils into the water.

Right. Two of Gilbert Jenkins's favourite plants were catmint and lavender, lavishly used at Great Fosters beneath the colonnade and in the parterre, and here beneath the arches of the rose garden.

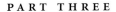

PART THREE

Designing, Building and Planting a Pergola

PAUL EDWARDS

Gourds have been planted ornamentally (and, it seems, for practical use as well) since Roman times. Columella (*On Agriculture*, X, 378ff) wrote:

> *...the twisted cucumber*
> *And the swelling gourd, sometimes from arbours hang,*
> *Sometimes, like snakes beneath the summer sun,*
> *Through the cool shadow of the grass do creep.*
> *Nor have they all one form: now, if you desire*
> *The longer shape which hangs from slender top,*
> *Then from the narrow neck select your seed;*
> *But if a gourd of globelike form you seek,*
> *Which vastly swells with ample maw, then choose*
> *A seed from the mid-belly, bearing fruit*
> *Which makes a vessel for Narycian pitch*
> *Or Attic honey from Hymettus' mount,*
> *Or handy water-pail or flask for wine;*
> *'Twill also teach the boys in pools to swim.*

Here the gourds are trained over an
iron tunnel arbour at Helmingham Hall in Suffolk.

PAUL EDWARDS

Elements of Design

The stone well-head acts as a focal point to the long rustic pergola at Polesden Lacey in Surrey.

Luxuriant rose blossom repays good cultivation on the brick and timber pergola at the Royal National Rose Society's Gardens of the Rose in St Albans, Hertfordshire.

A structure like a pergola will be a notable feature in the garden and great care should be taken about how it is sited. It needs to be an integral part of the layout and not something introduced for its own sake. Sir Edwin Lutyens, a master of the Arts and Crafts movement in domestic architecture and associated gardens, used pergolas as a protecting element in some of his schemes. Hestercombe House shows this idea (pages 78-83). Here a fine pergola terminates the southern boundary and is elevated above the adjoining field by a retaining wall. It gives a protecting feel to the walk and at the same time a good viewing platform to the rural landscape on one side and over the formal garden on the other. On a much larger scale the same idea of protection was used by Thomas Mawson in the garden for The Hill, overlooking Hampstead Heath (pages 84-89). In addition to this protecting role, a pergola can often be used as a way of defining spaces and thereby create rooms or separate areas in the layout, as at Wolfson College, Cambridge (pages 136-39).

Arches, too, make strong visual statements, either as single eye-catching features, or in defining spaces by being placed at regular intervals along a path. The style of the arch can vary from a simple structure to support a climbing plant over a path or arbour to a fully developed architectural design. The architectural arch is probably best suited to a large scale setting and will be built in masonry, but where conditions are favourable, impressive arches with much architectural character can be grown as topiary work (page 157).

With smaller properties and the contemporary practice of living more in the garden, paved terraces, patios and garden rooms are designed to be used for a variety of domestic functions. A small pergola in these situations will provide some seclusion, welcome shade on hot days, as well as the charms and fragrance of the climbing plants.

With its strong perspective vista, a pergola directs the eye and frames the view. The view could be to an interesting distant landscape or to a fountain or sculptural object in the garden. With such a strong perspective, a pergola or tunnel arbour should be on level ground, otherwise the steps or ramps will interfere with the view from within. With both pergolas and tunnel arbours everything in the structure needs to have precise alignment both horizontally and vertically. The carpenters working on the timber tunnel arbour in the Painswick Rococo Garden constantly used a surveyor's level to ensure that everything aligned correctly during its construction on site (page 145).

As with a colonnade, a pergola has a powerful rhythm of regularly spaced piers or columns, emphasised by the alternating pattern of light and shade falling across its central path. This quality is one of the delights of a pergola and obviously it needs to be in an open sunlit situation if this effect is to be fully realised. On the other hand tunnels of foliage casting a deep shade can be an effective and contrasting feature in the garden. Evergreens such as ivy have been popular, but trees, notably lime, are often trained to metal supports. There is a full description of one such tunnel on pages 152-55. False perspective can create very useful illusions of greater space in the garden when applied to such features as avenues, alleys and tunnel arbours. It is an underused stratagem.

The proportions for a pergola ought to ensure a comfortable walk for two people walking side by side, allowing for some lateral growth of the climbing plants. A roof height well clear of a tall person, plus hat, gives a comfortable and humanist feel to the structure. A successful standard is for the columns or piers to be some 2.5 metres (8 foot) apart in both directions, and some 2.8 to 3.0 metres (9 to 10 foot) high.

Above. Part of the extensive range of pergolas designed by Thomas Mawson for The Hill (see pages 84-89). This view shows the open timber roofed pavilion which is the meeting point of some of the arms of the pergolas. Note the fine architectural detailing to the timber superstructure.

A base supporting a square pier of the pergola at Hestercombe designed by Sir Edwin Lutyens (see pages 78-83). Lutyens used local rough split stone which contrasted with the ashlar Ham stone used for the orangery. The pretty long flowering daisy is *Erigeron karvinskianus* (formerly *E. mucronatus*).

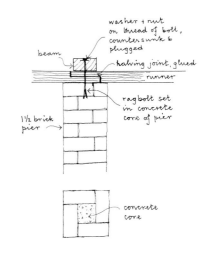

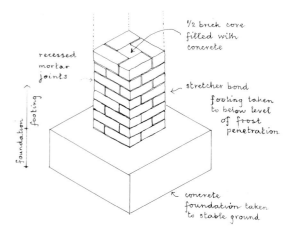

Right. **Construction of the top and base of a brick pier for a pergola.**

Stone and brick pergolas

The most substantial pergolas will have columns or piers in masonry – stone, brick, or brick and tile – with good quality construction and detailing. Successful designs have used classical columns, piers made from small brick sizes, rounded bricks to form cylindrical piers, often alternating with square ones. With brickwork, high quality bricks which are frostproof and of an even size should be used. These will allow for narrow courses of mortar and perhaps recessed pointing to show off the fine appearance of the bricks. For most pergolas a pier built with one and a half bricks on each side will look right, being neither too large nor too slender for the purpose. This arrangement will leave a centre core which can be filled with concrete and have a holding bolt cast into its summit for fixing timber beams and runners (see illustrations here and enlarged on page 160).

Radial bricks are used to build a round pier. They are bricks shaped to a segmental curve with angled ends all to a common radius. They are readily available from a number of brick suppliers, in a range of brick colours. Other brick manufacturers will fairly quickly make them as a special order.

With stone classical columns, care must be taken to ensure that they are correctly formed and proportioned, whether they are made especially for a project (expensive), or bought as artificial stone from a reputable manufacturer, or made in stucco to a brick core. The essential characteristic of nearly all classical columns is that they have a base and capital, and, joining the two, a column shaft with optical correction in its shaping, known as entasis. The optical illusion given by straight-sided columns makes them look concave. Entasis of the column shafts corrects this for the viewer. It is done by having the bottom third of the shaft cylindrical and therefore with vertical sides, while the remaining two thirds gently taper to the capital.

Fine classical buildings will have their column shafts made from one piece of stone, rendered stucco to give that appearance, or they will be made from large sections, finely jointed to look monolithic. A more relaxed attitude can be taken for pergolas as it is better for the garden to reflect

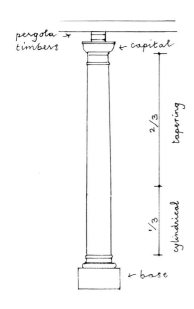

Drawing to show entasis to shaft of Tuscan column.

the region it is in. If this is stone country where the strata do not allow large pieces to be quarried, then the garden should follow the local use of stone. This was very much the case at Hestercombe, where relatively small stone was used to create the columns.

The use of stone has increased markedly in recent years, giving rise to the opening of new quarries, more local choice and, most importantly, a skilled workforce. In many countries there is a national organisation of approved suppliers and masons. In the United Kingdom it is the Stone Federation of Great Britain, who will be pleased to give advice.

The columns of a pergola will not be as well secured as those in a building where they will be supporting further masonry and are therefore firmly held to the perpendicular. As part of a pergola columns need to be well secured – with stainless steel dowels for example – to sound foundations and the tops of the columns also need to be well fixed to timber beams and runners to ensure as much stability as possible. Brick piers will need similar care to make sure they stay perpendicular, although the brickwork will often have a greater mass and so will have more inbuilt stability.

Timber pergolas

Timber can also be successfully used for the columns or posts, especially where a lighter or less grand structure seems appropriate. The timber posts will be most vulnerable to decay at their bases. The answer is either to use timber that is very durable and resistant to decay, or to keep the posts supported out of the ground. A stone base supporting the timber post well clear of the ground is a proven method. The stone or concrete base must rest on a secure foundation and have a recess at its top to take the post, which is also secured with a dowel. Once the post is fixed the recess should be sealed to prevent water getting in (see ill.). A newer method of supporting the timber post out of the ground is to have a metal shoe that wraps round the base of the post and has a bolt fixing. The shoe is well set into a concrete base and foundation.

Square timber posts look best in a pergola if they are given a planed finish. For added refinement the corners, at least at the entrances, can have stop chamfers. Most effective is where the

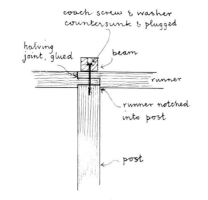

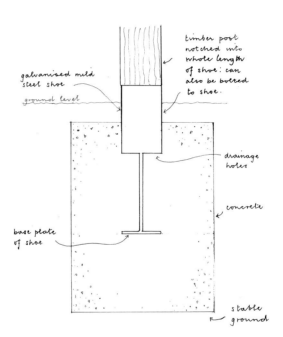

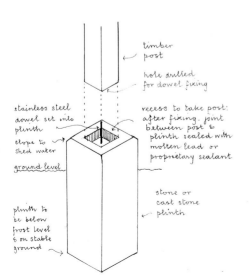

chamfered area equals the shaft part of a classical column, leaving the unchamfered top and bottom portions to equate with the capital and base (see ill.).

The superstructure or open roof of the pergola will normally be of timber, preferably a good hardwood for strength and longevity. It is made up of cross members, known as beams, and longitudinal pieces running along the sides of the roof over the posts or piers, called runners. The beams, especially if they are very substantial, are sometimes given a slightly arched configuration, following the classical concept of countering optical illusions, in this case of horizontals appearing to the eye to sag. The ends of the beams and runners should overhang well clear of the posts or piers and be given

Top centre. **Top of timber pergola showing jointing.**

Lower centre. **A design for a metal shoe to support and reduce decay of timber posts for pergola or arch; some metal fabricators have their own proprietary designs.**

Lower left. **Plinth support for timber pergola.**

Below. **Stop champfers to timber posts of pergola on two sides, but all four could be champfered.**

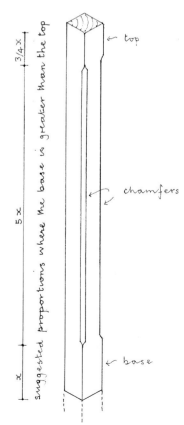

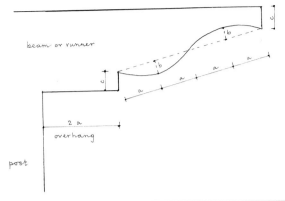

Left. Drawing showing cyma recta moulding to ends of beams and runners of pergola.

Centre. The top of the timber pergola at the Hunting Lodge, Warwick Castle Park (see pages 144-47), showing cyma recta profiles to ends of beams, chamfered inner edge to posts and jointing.

Bottom. One arm of the timber pergola in its romantic but domestic setting at the Hunting Lodge.

attractive and functional profiles. These will be very visible and it is a missed opportunity if, as is sometimes seen, the ends are simply cut off. For classically inspired pergolas the most aesthetically pleasing and functional profile is the cyma recta moulding (cyma = wave-like, recta = right or correct) as against the other well used profile, the cyma reversa, in which the wave-like shape is reversed.

Further but thinner timber pieces can be added to the pergola roof and notched into the beams to run the whole length of the structure, or,

alternatively, cables taken through the beams can be used to give more support for the climbing plants. Stainless steel cables are to be preferred. These can then have tensioners at the ends which will make for easy adjustments to the state of tension required.

Swags

Chains and ropes are sometimes fixed between the piers or posts of pergolas to become festooned with climbing plants. Sufficient slack is left to resemble a classical swag of flowers and foliage. Chains and ropes are usually attached to the piers or posts by metal hooking devices and rope ends can be given a decorative knot. Swept rails (metal

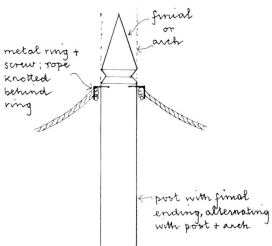

finial or arch

metal ring + screw; rope knotted behind ring

← post with finial ending, alternating with post + arch

Drawing showing top of post and fixing of ropes to support swags of roses or other climbers.

Left. Katherine Swift's larch posts and rope swags with roses at the back of her Victorian rose border at the Dower House, Morville Hall, Shropshire.

Timber posts supporting rope swags and roses at the restored Jekyll gardens at Upton Grey, Hampshire. The roses are 'Paul Transon' and 'Goldfinch'.

rods shaped to the required curve) can carry out the same function with the added advantage in some cases of giving lateral support to the posts (see pages 148-51).

Arches and arbours

The arbours shown in medieval illustrations were, as Sylvia Landsberg has shown (pages 21ff), built in wood. The grander ones were constructed in good carpentry work but for more modest situations they were more likely to have been made from coppice poles with infills of split poles forming a latticework. Contemporary accounts record that these structures would be fairly regularly repaired. The medieval arbour often enclosed a turf seat with latticework partly enclosing the back and sides and covered in summer with climbing plants. Larger arbours consisted of tunnels and domes and other elaborations.

Then as now the purpose of these timber arbours was to give privacy, shade and shelter from the wind. In summer they became a dark tunnel of foliage. Sometimes they were planted with fruit trees which were then trained over the structure. Both covered walks and arbour seats have remained popular features in the garden but a number of timber tunnel arbours have been destroyed or badly damaged by high winds or the combined forces of snow loading and exceptionally severe gusts of wind. Extra strength to combat such forces can be given by increasing the number and size of the posts and letting more of the wind flow through the structure by allowing, for example, some window openings. Care should also be taken to make sure the roof is not covered in

Above. Metal arches fixed to wooden posts form this circular rose arbour in the walled garden at Mottisfont Abbey in Hampshire where the national collection of old-fashioned roses is held.

Left. A series of arches supporting trained apple trees make this wonderful apple tunnel at Heale House in Wiltshire.

rampant foliage in winter as a build-up of snow could be fatal.

Once metal had become relatively easy to manufacture it was much used in the making of arches and arbours. Wrought iron was used to begin with, but this is now only available in limited quantity and sizes. It has been mainly replaced by mild steel, which has greater tensile strength but corrodes more quickly. Mild steel must therefore be protected from rusting and the most satisfactory method is hot-dip galvanising. This is carried out after fabrication by plunging the steelwork into molten zinc. This treatment should be specified for most garden work. It should be noted that the term ironwork tends to cover all forms of the metal, including alloys such as steel. With structural work of the type seen in lattice beams,

transmission towers or pylons, for example, it is a good idea to arrange the bracing struts in triangles. A triangle is a stronger shape than a rectangle. Cross bracing that also makes diamond shapes can be made much stronger by having the crossings welded or riveted together (see pages 152-55).

Metal arbours can be given elegant buttress supports to counter the danger of collapse from high winds (see pages 148-151). Posts of metal or wood should be taken well into the earth and rest on satisfactory load-bearing ground. Exact dimensions will depend on site conditions. With ironwork the foot of the posts should have base metal plates (see page 151). These plates must rest on firmly prepared footings in the excavated hole and the material for back filling should be returned and consolidated by ramming a little at a time to

ensure a firm support. Similar treatment will be needed for timber posts, but without base plates as the timber itself will be of a more substantial section.

The floor

The floor to a pergola or arbour will usually consist of a central path edged on both sides with narrow borders for the climbing plants. For pergolas the beds will often be wider, say two to three feet (60-90cm) to take additional planting of low shrubs and perennials. A good arrangement is to have about a third of the width of the bed between the line of the piers and the path. The path should be laid to a cross camber to allow surface water to run quickly into the plant beds. Any edging to the path should be left flush with the paving so as not to trap the water. This will also make it easier for any ground cover planting to spill out and give a soft edge to the path.

The pathway down a pergola should be somewhat special in its surfacing. Matching the stone or brick of the piers will give a pleasing unity to the scene. Small scale paving units usually look best in what is a small enclosed space. With brick paving it is worth looking at the opportunity to create a pattern that links to the piers and their regular spacing (see page 143). Laying bricks on their edge is a little extravagant, but the smaller scale effect is very rewarding and a welcome change from the ubiquitous block paving of urban areas. The type of brick needs to be of a quality that will not be damaged by freezing conditions. These are usually known as 'frost free'. Good quality bricks of this nature will look more attractive if they are laid without mortar joints. Instead they can be closely butted together with coarse sand brushed into the

An open timber roofed arbour acting as an eyecatcher at Greys Court, Oxfordshire.

A fine brick path and colourful
border lead to the pergola at
Barrington Court in Somerset.

joints for stability. The outer courses of the brick-work should be set and haunched in mortar to restrict lateral movement of the whole path. With this method of construction the colour of the brick is better shown and the drainage will be quicker, keeping the bricks drier.

Stone paving is also better laid in this way in the garden. The best architectural effect will come from using coursed slab paving of a type matching that used in the piers or columns. In some areas the nature of the local stone may mean that crazy paving is in keeping with the vernacular style.

Crazy paving will usually need mortar joining, unless a lot of cutting of the stone is acceptable. The mortar should match the colour of the stone as closely as possible. If necessary stone dust can be used in the mortar mix.

Arbour seats and tunnels are less strongly architectural in character and gravel can be a suitable choice for their floors. However this is an opportunity to experiment with many other small scale materials, such as pebbles and slate or tiles laid on edge, to make interesting and unique floor patterns.

Plants and Planting

Climbing plants

Nature, with an occasional helping hand from man, has given us an enormous and varied range of plants ideal for pergolas or arbours. The structures themselves, if well designed, not only complement the beauty of the plants but also make the best possible support on which to display this great variety of flowers, fruit and foliage.

Climbing plants have evolved a number of ways of supporting their growth as they climb towards the light. The different methods have an important bearing on the type of help they need if they are to give good cover to the structures.

First there are the twiners that spiral and twist their way round suitable objects. Wisteria and honeysuckle are in this category and they may need some initial help to attach themselves to large columns or piers. Then come those plants, notably clematis, that climb by way of sensitive leaf stalks. When they come in contact with something that can be grasped they will twine round it and take a firm hold. Other climbers have developed string-like growths called tendrils that also readily twine and attach themselves to objects of small diameter. Both these latter types of climber will need some minor support like netting or tying-in with string as the main growth develops.

Some other climbing plants – rambler roses are the obvious example – use hooked prickles to scramble over surrounding plants or objects. The new growths of these scramblers will need to be tied and trained along the structure.

Yet another group of climbers have adhesively tipped tendrils or aerial roots that attach themselves to most surfaces. Virginia creeper is a prime example. Finally there are the climbers like *Hydrangea petiolaris* and ivies that use aerial roots or rootlets which grow into any small crevices and take a firm hold.

Climbers for flowers

Climbers which have notable flowers are the most important plants for pergolas and arbours, and among them are our most prized garden flowers.

Wisterias are much associated with pergolas and their long racemes hang spectacularly down from the roof of the structure. In his comprehensive work in four volumes, *Trees and Shrubs hardy in the British Isles*, W.J.Bean wrote of the Chinese wisteria, *Wisteria sinensis*, 'No other climber ever brought to this country has added more to the beauty of gardens'. It is very strong growing and capable of covering large trees. The flowers are mauve to deep purple and fragrant. There are several forms including a good white one. However, it develops a massive trunk for a climber and therefore needs either a very strong structure, or very careful management, or both.

Wisteria floribunda from Japan will often be more suitable for the limited space of most pergolas. Its flowers are violet or purplish-blue and fragrant. This species, unlike other wisterias, has stems that turn clockwise, which makes it easy to identify when not in flower. There are several different coloured forms and the much admired *Wisteria floribunda* 'Multijuga' (*Wisteria floribunda* 'Macrobotrys') which has very long racemes, best seen when they can drop from a pergola or high arch over a bridge, as favoured in some Japanese gardens.

Wisterias are rampant growers when once established. They should be pruned twice a year on a pergola, otherwise they will deteriorate into a tangled mass with few flowers. The first pruning must be of the current year's lateral growth to shorten the shoots to about 150mm (6 inches). This should be done towards the end of July or early August. In December or January the same shoots are further shortened to about two buds.

Climbing and rambler roses give the best value in terms of flowers considering how little ground they occupy. It is not surprising they are so popular for both pergolas and arbours. Generally the climbing roses have fewer and stiffer stems but larger individual flowers. Ramblers have smaller flowers but in large clusters and more new but rather whippy growth from the base. Climbers and ramblers of a more moderate stature are often called pillar roses and, as the name suggests, are suitable for pillars and pergolas. Many climbing roses will repeat their flowering later in the summer, whereas the ramblers pack everything into one most glorious riot of bloom in late June and into July. The number of roses is enormous and perhaps the best way to begin choosing is to visit some good rose gardens and nurseries.

The taller growing roses are best avoided as it is not a good idea to swamp the pergola. On the other hand roses that hang their flowers down are just the thing for arches and arbours. One of the best of these is the rambler 'Adélaide d'Orléans', with its creamy-white, semi-double flowers held in elegant sprays. Climbing roses that flower prolifically and repeat well include 'New Dawn', 'Iceberg'. 'Golden Showers' and 'Handel'.

Banksian roses are grouped with ramblers. They need very warm situations in Britain to survive cold winters. In northern Italy they are a popular choice for large arbours, sometimes covering quite extensive outdoor eating places. The flowers develop on hanging sprays in May on second or third year's growth and so should not be pruned, except for removal of old wood. *Rosa banksiae* var. *banksiae* has small white flowers with a very strong fragrance of violets.

Climbing roses should be pruned annually to remove main growths that are old and deteriorating or are simply too plentiful. Side shoots which have flowered in the previous season should be cut back to 50 to 75 mm (2-3 inches). Ramblers only need the minimum of pruning, apart from the removal of old main growths from time to time. It is often a good plan to train in new growth in a spiral round an upright support to encourage flowering along the whole length of the stem.

Previous page. **Rambling roses like this 'American Pillar' are well supported on the timber roof beams at Hestercombe.**

Above. **A well pruned wisteria flowering over an open metal arbour at a café in Pienza, Italy.**

A climbing rose beginning to cover the rustic larch pergola at Polesden Lacey in Surrey.

Along with roses clematis must rank as one of the most important genera of climbing plants for the pergola and arbour. In his foreword to Ernest Markham's book *Clematis* published in 1935, William Robinson wrote, 'They are as hardy as the British Oak, as proved in my garden, come early into flower and only cease with the approach of winter; of few other flowers can this be said'. By 'they' he meant those clematis (the majority) that originated in the temperate region of the northern hemisphere.

Their long flowering season starts in late January with the evergreen *Clematis cirrhosa* var. *balearica* and its cultivars, followed by another evergreen, *Clematis armandii* and its cultivars, which flower in March and April with dazzling white or pink blossom and fragrance. These are followed in spring by hardier varieties such as *Clematis alpina* and *Clematis macropetala* and their cultivars, and the ever popular *Clematis montana* with its numerous varieties and cultivars. Some of these cultivars are scented – *Clematis montana* 'Elizabeth' has a delicious vanilla

fragrance. On into summer we have the many larger-flowered cultivars, *jackmanii* and *viticella* types, and the late-flowering species.

In general terms pruning is needed to remove dead wood, and shoots that have grown beyond the confines of the pergola should be shortened. If summer flowering clematis, particularly *jackmanii* types, are to flower well they should be hard pruned down to strong leaf axil buds in late February and early March.

The summer flowering jasmine (*Jasminum officinale*) has for several centuries been a great favourite in our gardens, covering cottage arbours and climbing up the more stately piers of pergolas. It thoughtfully follows the main flowering of rambler roses with its sweetly scented white flowers. There are several cultivars, the best of which is *Jasminum officinale* f. *affine*. *Jasminum* x *stephanense* has sweetly scented pale pink flowers and is equally suitable for pergolas. The young leaves are often variegated. *Jasminum nudiflorum*, the well known winter flowering jasmine, has bright yellow flowers but no scent. *Jasminum polyanthum* is now

a popular choice for Mediterranean climates as is vigorous, very floriferous and intensely fragrant.

Along with jasmines, the honeysuckles, with their sweetly scented flowers, are also much loved climbers for the pergola and arbour. *Lonicera periclymenum*, our native woodbine, is as good as any for fragrance. There are, as can be expected, many cultivars, giving earlier or later flowering and different colours. They will do well in some shade, but do not like dry conditions. The fact that the funnel-shaped flowers are pollinated by bumble bees during the day and by hawk moths at night shows that their fragrance can be enjoyed at any time of day or night.

A more rampant species is *Lonicera japonica*, which is also evergreen or, in cold winters, semi-evergreen. *Lonicera japonica* 'Halliana' is perhaps too vigorous for a pergola. The cultivar 'Aureoreticulata' has scented yellow flowers and beautiful golden reticulation in the leaves. *Lonicera japonica* and its cultivars flower on the current season's growth, so any clipping to keep them within bounds should be done in the spring.

For warm sheltered areas in Britain, two climbing solanums will provide an abundance of potato flowers from July on to October. *Solanum crispum* 'Glasnevin' has clusters of purple-blue flowers, while *Solanum laxum* 'Album' (formerly *Solanum jasminoides* 'Album') is white.

Another climber for milder areas is *Passiflora caerulea*, the passion flower. It is evergreen and has tendrils enabling it to climb very effectively. The well known flowers are spectacular and up to 10 cm (4 inches) across with a slight fragrance.

The silk vine, *Periploca graeca*, has long been grown here and was often recommended for pergolas. However it is not much seen in gardens today although it is still obtainable from some nurseries. It is a vigorous twining climber needing a sunny position. The flowers, which are produced from July to August, are brownish-purple with a greenish-yellow outside and a heavy odour.

Clematis and fuschia are the key plants on this metal tunnel arbour in the Victorian garden at Penrhyn Castle, Gwynedd, Wales.

Campis grandiflora, the trumpet vine, needs a warm wall to flourish in Britain, but in warmer climates it is a very good climber for pergolas with its large panicles of trumpet-shaped orange or red flowers. In the southern United States *Campis radicans* is a native climber and very suitable there for a pergola. It gives good shade and brilliant orange and scarlet flowers.

Two climbing annuals, grown for their flowers, can also be trained over arches and up posts and piers. Sweet peas, *Lathyrus*, have been bred to give a great range of colours and have a robustness that makes them suitable for this purpose. In warm and sunny situations, morning glory, *Ipomoea*, with the large trumpet flowers that close by the afternoon will reach some 3 metres (10 feet). Seedsmen list several colours, but 'Heavenly Blue' is still the best known.

Climbers for foliage

Ivy, *Hedera*, is a small genus, but with many cultivars giving a range of variegation, size and colouring of foliage. They are all evergreen, self-clinging by means of aerial roots, and will grow in any soil and climate in Britain. They will take hard clipping and are ideal for creating a dark tunnel arbour.

The ornamental vines are chiefly grown for their foliage and autumn colouring. *Vitis vinifera* 'Brant' has deeply lobed leaves that turn red and purple in the autumn. With good cultivation and a warm summer it will produce small, sweet, dark purple-black grapes. *Vitis vinifera* 'Purpurea' has foliage that starts a claret colour and turns later to a rich purple. *Vitis coignetiae* is the most spectacular with huge leaves that turn to the most brilliant crimson and scarlet in autumn. It is very vigorous

Timber posts and rope swags well covered with honeysuckle at the Exhedra garden in the Painswick Rococo Garden, Gloucestershire.

and will need severe pruning to keep it in place on a pergola or arbour.

The *Parthenocissus* family includes the well known Virginia creeper, *Parthenocissus quinque-folia* along with Boston ivy (*Parthenocissus tricuspidata*). Both are tall-growing, self-clinging climbers, noted for their brilliant autumn colouring. They are too rampant for pergolas, but can be used more successfully over very large arbours as, for example, over an out-of-doors eating area. The smaller growing *Parthenocissus henryana* is a better choice for the pergola. The silvery-white to pink veining of its leaves is most attractive in the spring and summer months and then again as it turns red in the autumn. It grows and looks best when planted away from the sun.

Celastrus scandens is a vigorous twining climber. It is mainly grown for the good yellow autumn colouring of its leaves, which contrasts so well with the orange seeds which are exposed and held in their capsules.

Humulus lupulus 'Aurea', golden hop, has large leaves of an attractive soft yellow. It is suitable for pergolas and arbours and grows best in full sun.

Climbers for fruit and vegetables

The early pergolas of Italy were very much for growing the fruiting vine. When mature the vine has very strong stems or canes that can be trained to cover a vast area as is famously demonstrated by the huge 'Black Hamburg' grape grown under glass at Hampton Court Palace. If they are to grow well vines need much checking of growth and pruning and the variety must be suited to the local climate. In Britain vines trained on a pergola are less likely to fruit well compared with those trained against a warm wall or grown as low shrubs close to the radiating heat from the ground in a vineyard.

Some vegetables, runner beans in particular, can be grown as climbing annuals and with their attractive red or white flowers followed by fresh green pods for the kitchen can twine their way up into arbours very effectively. Ornamental gourds can be grown in the same way. The arbour will be bare for much of the year, but a strong design, perhaps with an ogee outline, will more than compensate.

Trees and shrubs

As well as such plants as are natural climbers there are a number of trees and shrubs which can be very successfully trained. The trees which are used for pleached hedges, notably limes and hornbeam, are the ones most often used to make tunnels of foliage. Evergreen arbours can be made by training yew over them. The golden forms of yew are always good value and one of the best is *Taxus baccata* 'Elegantissima' with its ascending branches.

Any plant that has its flowers hanging down, such as those with racemes, can often be wonderfully displayed in arbours and pergolas. Laburnums are spectacular when used in this way.

Scarlet runner beans provide bright summer foliage, red flowers and delicious vegetables. Here they twine over a metal tunnel arbour at Helmingham Hall, Suffolk.

Well pruned apple trees in flower along the metal tunnel arbour at Heale House, Wiltshire. The apple and pear tunnels at Heale were planted as maidens by Lady Anne Rasch in 1965.

Laburnum x *watereri* 'Vossii' with its more erect growth and its very long racemes of scented yellow flowers is especially recommended. All the seeds of laburnum are poisonous, but this hybrid has the merit of producing fewer of them. With the right husbandry laburnum tunnels make one of the most spectacular floral displays for the garden and amply reward care in their initial training and annual pruning. All the work should be carried out from late summer to midwinter; any later runs the risk of bleeding from the rising sap. To begin with the laburnums should be planted along both sides of the tunnels about 2-3 metres (6-10 feet) apart. In the first season new growth should be tied to cover the structure. Where necessary lead-ing shoots should be pruned back to encourage new laterals to ensure a well spaced coverage of the tunnel. Once this has been achieved prune annually to reduce the density of the growth and foliage and to promote the formation of clusters of flower buds, known as spurs. At the same time remove dead wood and allow new growth to fill in any gaps in the coverage. The unwanted current year's growth should then be pruned back to two or three buds to encourage spur formation.

Fruit trees, such as apples, pears and quinces, can be trained to cover arches and arbours and have a double bonus – blossom in the spring and fruit in the autumn. Care must be taken with apples and pears either to plant self fertile varieties or to make sure there is the right mix for successful cross pollination. It is also important to choose the best rootstock in relation to the size of arbour or arch to be covered. A good fruit grower's catalogue will give the relevant information. Where the climate is suitable arbours planted with citrus trees are a delight and have the added pleasure of the highly scented flowers.

Some shrubs which were introduced to Great Britain in the last two centuries would seem to be potential candidates for arbours. *Magnolia sieboldii* subsp. *sinensis* and *Magnolia wilsonii*, with their hanging flowers and wonderfully exotic scent, ought to be tried out in this way. When fuschias are grown in hanging baskets we can appreciate their flowers to best advantage. Tall growing fuschias were often trained to one or more stems and taken over the walkway in conservatories so that the flowering could be the better enjoyed. In suitable climates – mild and wet – they would be most successful trained over arches and arbours. The tall growing shrub abutilons which produce their hanging flowers over a long period would also be an exciting experimental choice. *Buddleia asiatica* has long heavily scented panicles and would be most pleasing, but it needs a warm climate. It is time to experiment.

On a recent visit to Salzburg I was intrigued to discover what was trained over the long and wide tunnel arbour in the Mirabellgarten. It was not obvious from a distance but it turned out to be a tall growing philadelphus. Its flowers mainly show on the outside of the arbour rather than inside, but I was told that this is more than made up for by the ravishing scent which fills the arbour walk during high summer. A tall mock orange, such as *Philadelphus delavayi* or *Philadelphus tomentosus* 'Virginal', would be the first requirement. Pruning would consist of removing old flowering shoots back to the new growths which can then be tied on to the arbour structure. At the Mirabellgarten this was in ironwork.

Training trees and shrubs for arbours will always mean tying in new growth and in some cases reducing the number of main branches. The annual growth that will need to be cut back on potentially large trees will be considerable, especially at the roof of the arbour. Yew trees can be clipped like yew hedges and the leading shoots left untouched until they have reached the required length. Apple and pear trees will need to be pruned in the same way as cordons or espaliers to ensure that the trees are kept to the required number of branches. These branches must be encouraged to develop spurs with flower buds and for this summer and winter pruning will be needed. The summer pruning should be carried out in mid-July with the shoots cut back to 150mm (6 inches) of their base. In the winter the shoots should again be cut back – this time to two or so buds. Fuller instructions are readily available in books on fruit growing. Flowering trees and shrubs should also be restricted as to the number of branches allowed to develop and should be given some pruning to encourage spurs with flower buds.

Planting for living arbours

The art of weaving growths of living trees into screens and arbours has become very popular. All the trees, such as limes, *Tilia*, hornbeam, *Carpinus betulus*, and hazel *Corylus avellana*, traditionally used for pleached hedges, are suitable, but the most commonly used today is willow, which can be easily rooted on the spot from cuttings and makes very flexible growths for weaving. All the willows are suitable bar the aptly named crack willow, *Salix fragilis*, which is too brittle. For arbours it is best to choose strong growing willows such as the common osier, *Salix viminalis*, or, if coloured stems seem a good idea, *Salix daphnoides* (violet), *Salix purpurea* (purple) or *Salix alba* subsp. *vitellina* (golden).

The willows can be set to grow on the actual site for the arbour by inserting rods and smaller cuttings well into the ground and keeping them watered until well rooted. The smaller cuttings are set and grown at an angle so that they can be woven into latticework panels. Tarred twine is used to secure them together at the crossing points. As the willow grows the stems will enlarge and tighten the fixing, causing the cambium of the two stems to fuse together and so giving greater strength to the structure. Pruning is done in the winter when unwanted growth is taken back to some three buds.

There are now a number of experienced people in this field who give demonstrations of the

A living willow arbour and seat in the wild garden at Upton Grey, Hampshire.

various techniques and can also undertake the work for you (see also pages 67-68).

Underplanting

Arbours are usually densely planted, leaving little room or light for underplanting. The traditional pergola, with its regular spaces between the piers, more readily accommodates underplanting. This best takes the form of beds bordering each side of the central path. On the whole the planting is best kept low. It can either give one glorious display coinciding with the main flowering of the climbers (blue irises under wisteria, for example), or the display can be extended. As the pergola is essentially to be strolled through at leisure, scented flowers will be much enjoyed.

In most cases the pergola will be used throughout the year and the owner will want all year round interest from the underplanting. I would start with snowdrops, that supremely rewarding and undemanding bulb, which begins to show itself in January and is unsurpassed in February. The smaller daffodils and *Dicentra formosa* and its excellent cultivars could make the next succession. Lilies of the valley, *Convallaria majalis* and cultivars, make a fine ground covering plant with beautiful flowers and superb fragrance in May followed by good maintenance-free foliage throughout the summer. In early summer the garden pinks give colour and fragrance to the pergola walk. *Dianthus* 'Mrs Sinkins' was traditionally a great favourite for the underplanting of pergolas. Today many gardeners prefer 'White Ladies' which is equally fragrant, less blowsy and has more glaucous foliage. There are many other cultivars and species that are suitable. Clove carnations flower later in the summer and have good colours and that most powerful and unmistakable fragrance. The presence of white lilies on a still evening will be memorable.

Irises, in particular the *Iris germanica* cultivars, are an essential part of most early summer displays; their vertical sword-like foliage making a

pleasing contrast and punctuation in the mass of surrounding planting. It is best to avoid the taller growing cultivars as these will not always be self-supporting in this situation. In good fertile soils the Lady's Mantle, *Alchemilla mollis*, also flowers in early summer with feathery sprays of greenish yellow and its attractive foliage makes a good ground cover for the whole season. The smaller lavenders are excellent for high summer displays, along with golden marjoram, *Origanum vulgare* 'Aureum'. This useful culinary herb produces flowers that are rich in nectar and so will be constantly visited by working bees. Autumn ought to be marked by the flowering of the autumn crocus, *Colchicum autumnale*, and the dainty hardy cyclamen, *C. hederifolium*.

As well as the more permanent planting, some bedding plants, such as wallflowers, tulips and sweet williams, can be added to the borders where space has been left for annual planting. Initially some annuals could well be sown along the borders to fill them up temporarily until the permanent planting takes over. Love-in-the-mist, *Nigella damascena*, readily germinates and seeds itself into any available open space to ensure its welcome survival for many future seasons.

An altogether different approach would be to have the underplanting consist mostly of foliage plants. These could be hostas with their wide range of leaf colouring and shape; the bold and evergreen leaves of bergenias; or ferns, ornamental grasses and silvery artemisias.

Principles of cultivation

All the plants chosen to cover an arbour or pergola should be planted as close to the posts or piers as possible, in holes which are big enough to spread out the roots. Any compaction of the subsoil should be broken up to ensure good drainage. Special attention to help the plant become established in its new situation is vital. This may mean mulching on dry soils, watering during dry spells

Hostas and ferns thriving in the more shady part of the underplanting in the pergola at West Dean, Sussex.

and early training of the plant to the structure. Subsequent cultivation will include any necessary pruning, training feeding and measures to counter any attacks from pests and diseases. Specialist information on, for example, roses or clematis, will give advice on how to cultivate these specific groups of plants. Here we must confine ourselves to general principles. A person who is successful with plants is often described as having 'green fingers'. In reality this means having a strong empathy for plants and their well being. The earliest signs of stress, or attacks from pests or diseases, are noticed, prompting helpful action.

Nevertheless, there may be times when the wrong plant is simply in the wrong place and for a variety of possible reasons will not flourish. It may be that a particular rose is susceptible to mildew in adverse conditions, such as dry soils in sheltered situations, and consequently looks disfigured for much of the summer. In such circumstances replacement should be seriously considered, whether with another type of climber, or another rose known for its resistance to mildew. If the latter is chosen then it is essential to replace the soil in and around the planting hole to avoid 'rose sickness'.

A garden is more a process than something fixed and static and so good continuous cultivation is the key to having a fine garden. As with human relationships, there must be giving as well as taking.

Roses, under expert care, flowering in profusion over the pergola at the Royal National Rose Society's Gardens of the Rose, St Albans, Hertfordshire.

Six Design Projects

PAUL EDWARDS

A detail of the pediment of Paul Edwards's rustic yew arch at
Hidcote Manor Garden, Gloucestershire.

Brick and Timber Pergola

In its fully developed architectural form, when regularly spaced masonry piers or columns support a substantial timber superstructure, the pergola can be used to define and enclose spaces in both urban and landscape design. When Lee Court was built in 1995 the southern side was left unenclosed as there was not enough room for another building. The lack of definition to the space was a major concern in considering the landscape design for the court. As there was already a need for a path at this end the best solution seemed to be to build a pergola. This would give the necessary enclosure to the court and provide a pleasing walkway and garden feature.

The piers and the paving have the same brick types as the buildings, which helps to unite the pergola with the court. The piers are 1½ bricks square with a small central core which is filled with concrete. A metal bolt was fixed into the concrete at the top of

each pier to secure the timber superstructure (see page 160). The bricks are frost-proof, as they will nearly always need to be in such roofless structures subject to full exposure to the weather. Building free-standing brick piers is quite a test of bricklaying skills. Any deviation from the vertical will be very obvious and uncomfortable to the eye. The notable and well respected Cambridge firm of Rattee and Kent constructed this pergola and even they decided to put the work to their best bricklayers.

A very durable hardwood, iroko, has been used for the runners and beams and all the ends have cyma recta mouldings (see over and page 161). Stainless steel cables run through the cross beams to give further support for the climbing plants.

For something as special in the garden as a pergola it seems appropriate to think carefully about the paving. The paving material should relate to the masonry of the piers or columns. Two types of bricks have been used for the path here, one being the same as that used in the piers. The design is repeated in each area defined by four piers. The centre of the pattern is a square formed by bricks laid on edge with four joints crossing diagonally. This square is framed by a darker brick making up the overall rectangle between the four piers. The bricks laid on edge give a pleasing smaller scale to the design, appropriate in a garden as against the vaster expanse of say a shopping precinct. The path has been laid to a camber so that it not only stays dry but also usefully sheds rainwater to the side planting beds.

The ultimate aim is to have the whole pergola covered in Chinese wisteria (*Wisteria sinensis*). However one or two climbing roses were also planted to give some instant flowering in the short term. The side borders have been filled with flag irises (*Iris germanica* hybrids), mostly blue flowering to link up with the colour of the wisteria racemes above. This choice of planting means that there is only one full flowering each year during May and into June, but this is in the summer term when the gardens are most actively enjoyed.

BRICK AND TIMBER PERGOLA,
LEE COURT, WOLFSON COLLEGE, CAMBRIDGE

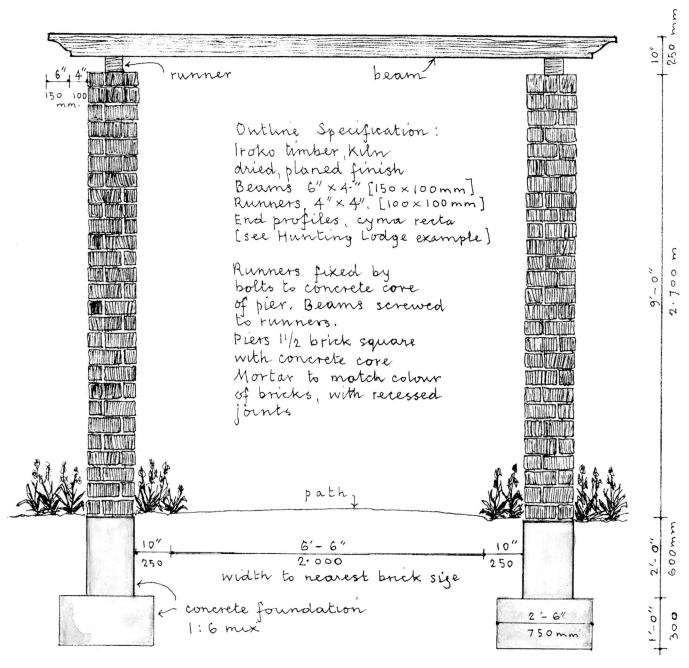

runner

beam

6" 4"
150 100
mm.

10"
250 mm

Outline Specification:
Iroko timber, kiln
dried, planed finish
Beams 6" × 4" [150 × 100 mm]
Runners 4" × 4" [100 × 100 mm]
End profiles, cyma recta
[see Hunting Lodge example]

Runners fixed by
bolts to concrete core
of pier. Beams screwed
to runners.
Piers 1½ brick square
with concrete core
Mortar to match colour
of bricks, with recessed
joints

9'-0"
2.700 m

path

10"
250

6'-6"
2.000

10"
250

width to nearest brick size

concrete foundation
1:6 mix

2'-6"
750 mm

2'-0"
600mm

1'-0"
300

Outline Specification
Bricks to be frost proof: joints filled
with 1:4 lime mortar on 1" [25 mm] mortar
bed on 3" [75 mm] well consolidated hardcore
Outer edges of paving haunched
        in concrete 1:2:4 mix.

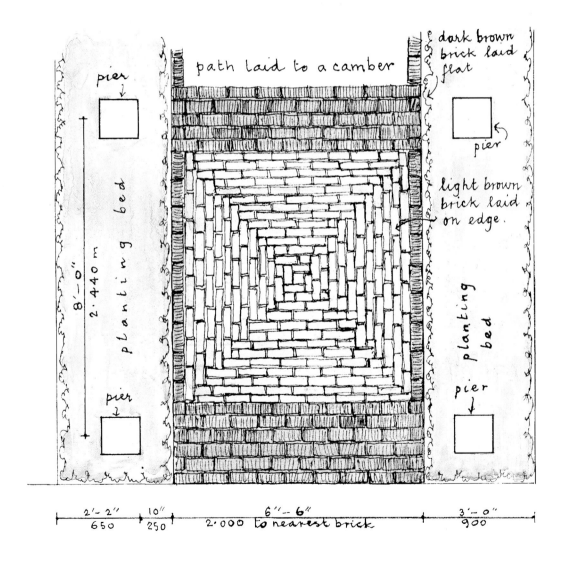

PLAN of BRICK PAVING PATTERN to PERGOLA

Timber Pergola Garden

When the new owner bought the property in the early 1980s the Hunting Lodge had become semi-derelict and the gardens very derelict. It was clear from the historical records for Warwick Castle that some fine formal gardens had been created at the Hunting Lodge in the early years of the twentieth century. The designs were drawn up by Harold Peto for Frances Evelyn, Countess of Warwick. Peto had worked extensively at her Essex home, Easton Lodge (see page 59).

All that remained in the pergola garden were some stone bases for supporting timber posts, and it was from these that the garden we have today evolved. The garden has four entrances from which four pergolas run up to the centre where they join up in an octagon. The focal points are therefore the four entrances and the centre of the octagon. In the latter we placed a purpose made baluster type sundial turned from Hornton stone. An iron seat was specially made to close one vista and a decorative gate

another. The entrance from the north has a fine view over the castle park.

The pergolas were built on artificial stone bases which were recessed to take the posts. These posts were secured with stainless steel dowels and the joint made waterproof with molten lead. The posts were given chamfers to the inner edges and the ends to the beams and runners given a good overhang with cyma recta profiles. All the timber is durable hardwood with wooden pegs to secure the joints.

A mixture of climbing plants, including roses, honeysuckle, clematis and summer jasmine, gives a long season of flowering. The owner had been impressed by the twenty-four 'The Garland' rambler roses planted in the recreated Victorian rose garden at the castle and so this rose was included in the selection. Low growing plants in narrow beds make for simple underplanting. These beds have a paved gap at each arm of the pergola to allow easy access to the adjoining garden enclosures.

TIMBER PERGOLA, HUNTING LODGE, WARWICK CASTLE PARK

Site: level & partly enclosed by hedges & retaining
wall with existing paths to Lodge & tower garden.

Outline Specification:
Iroko timber, kiln
dried, jointed &
pegged, & supported
on artificial stone
plinths & secured
by stainless steel
dowels, sealed
with molten lead
posts 5"× 5" [125 × 125 mm]
beams & runners 4"× 2½"
[100 × 62 mm]

n

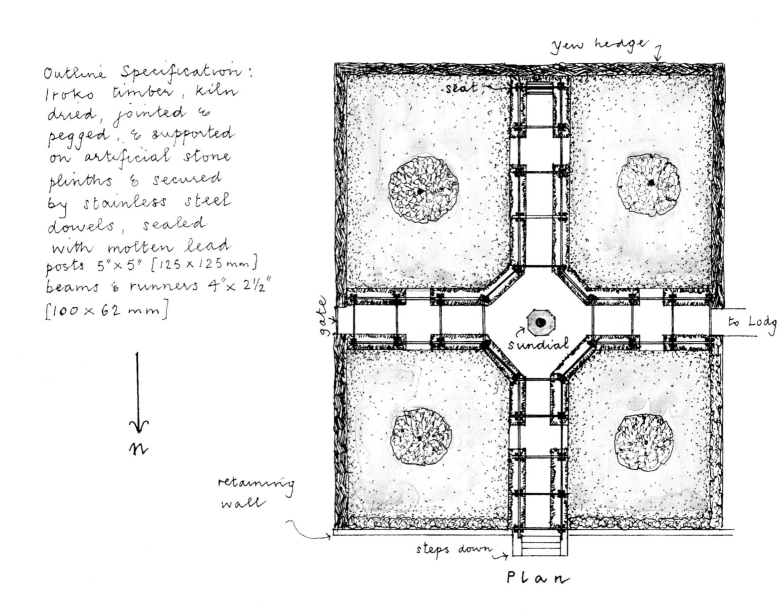

yew hedge

seat

gate

sundial

to Lodge

retaining
wall

steps down

Plan

runners notched over top
of post & beam & pegged

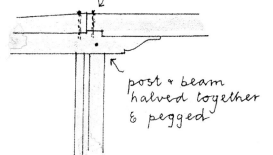

Detail of top of
octagon posts

Detail of shape of
octagon posts -
all to point to centre;
shaped from 5" × 5"
[125 × 125 mm]

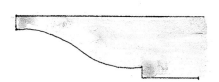

Detail of cyma recta
profile for ends of
beams & runners

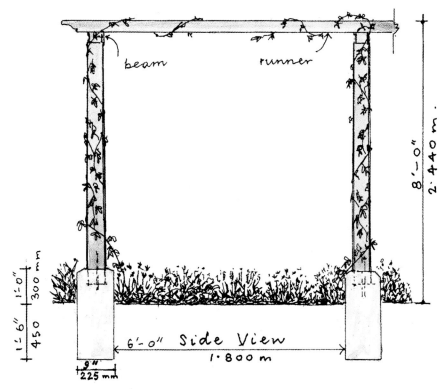

beam   runner

8'-0"
2·440 m

1'-0"   300 mm
1'-6"   450

6'-0" Side View
1·800 m

9"
225 mm

post & beam
halved together
& pegged

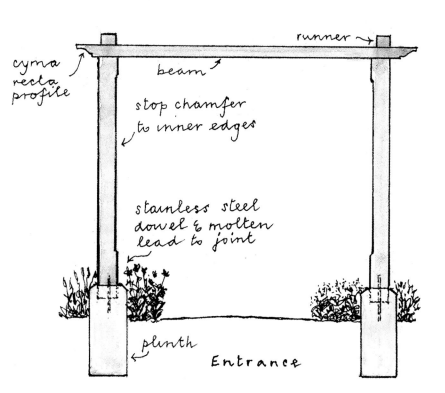

cyma
recta
profile

runner →

beam →

stop chamfer
to inner edges

stainless steel
dowel & molten
lead to joint

plinth

Entrance

Timber Tunnel Arbour

The garden at Painswick is a rare example of the Rococo style of gardening that flourished for a short while in the middle of the eighteenth century. Restoration began in 1986 and has now been largely completed. Fortunately, along with many other now lost examples, Painswick had been faithfully recorded in charming watercolour drawings by Thomas Robins. The panoramic view, dated 1748, proved to be very accurate and has been the major guide in the restoration. This painting shows a long tunnel arbour, curiously sited – but perhaps in keeping with the rather whimsical ideas of the Rococo – down one side of a fish pond.

Lord Dickinson, the owner, asked me for a design for a new tunnel arbour that would give as few maintenance problems as possible and was to be built to a strict budget. I decided on a timber construction, using iroko timber, which is very durable – it is used for wooden draining boards. The design involves 24 arches across the pathway with 23 arches running along each side. This means that three arches spring from each post, one to each side and one at right angles between them. It was essential, with a long tunnel like this, that all alignments were true – any variation would stand out like a sore thumb. The craftsmen (carpenters and joiners) had a surveyor's level permanently set up on site during the construction.

The arbour is mostly planted with *Laburnum anagyroïdes* (the common laburnum), but there is also some summer jasmine, honeysuckle and clematis to give a longer season of flowering. These three climbers would all have been available at the time of the original arbour.

TIMBER TUNNEL ARBOUR, PAINSWICK ROCOCO GARDEN

Outline Specification: Timber iroko, kiln dried, planed finish
All joints pegged and glued, except
top rail which is to be notched ½" [12mm]
into main arches; main & side arches
made from two pieces.
Timber sizes: posts 4" x 4" [100 x 100 mm]
main [cross] arches 4" x 2" [100 x 50 mm];
side arches 3" x 2" [75 x 50 mm];
top & side rails 2" x 2" [50 x 50 mm]

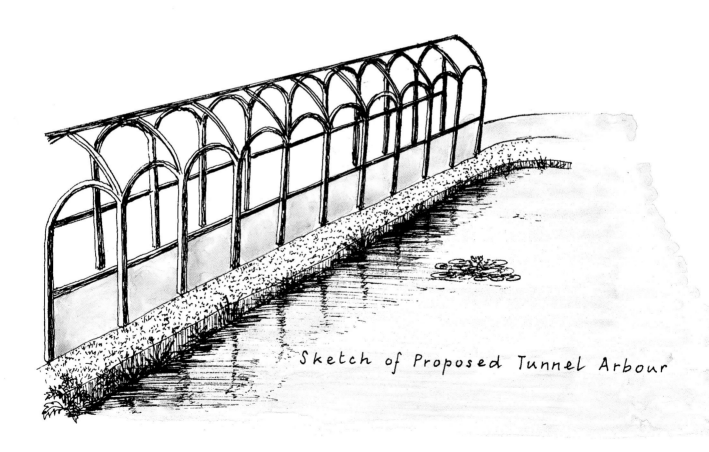

Sketch of Proposed Tunnel Arbour

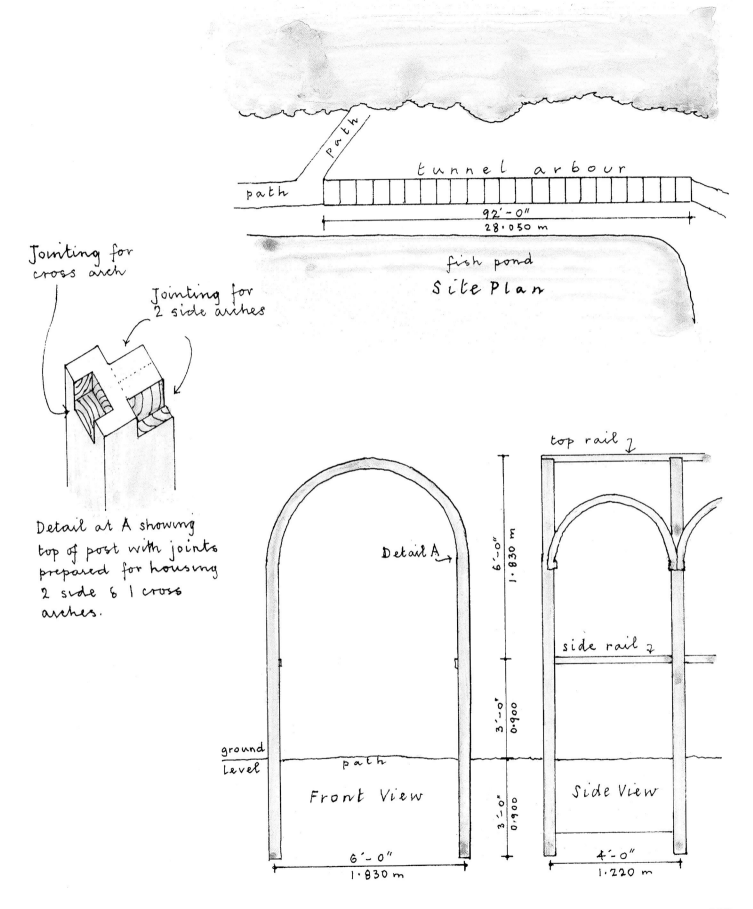

tunnel arbour

92'-0"
28.050 m

path

Path

path

fish pond

Site Plan

Jointing for
cross arch

Jointing for
2 side arches

Detail at A showing
top of post with joints
prepared for housing
2 side & 1 cross
arches.

Detail A →

top rail ↴

side rail ↴

6'-0"
1.830 m

3'-0"
0.900

3'-0"
0.900

ground
level

path

Front View

Side View

6'-0"
1.830 m

4'-0"
1.220 m

Iron Tunnel Arbour and Arches

The landscaping at Warwick Castle was one of Capability Brown's earliest and most admired commissions. However by the middle of the nineteenth century the then Earl of Warwick – like most country house owners of the time – wanted to introduce some formal flower gardens. A parterre flower garden and a rose garden were designed by Robert Marnock, a leading garden designer of the time and a friend of William Robinson. He exploited the new range of possibilities and made abundant use of ironwork.

The rose garden was made in 1868 but had disappeared by the end of the Second World War. Two surviving drawings by Marnock were found in the County Record Office and they formed the basis for a suggested recreation. The garden was officially opened by Diana, Princess of Wales, in July 1986.

The route to the garden from the castle was not fully shown on Marnock's drawing, but it clearly began with a number of arches. In the recreated garden the whole route was arched. Over time and with the robust growth of the roses the arches alone were not strong enough to withstand falls of snow and high winds. The final structure is now a fully developed iron tunnel arbour. Extra tubular steel arches have been added, each of the existing arches has been given four supporting side stays, and the roof has continuous lines of slats welded to the arches.

Each main arch is made up of two arch members which are fixed together by diagonal braces welded at their crossing points. These diagonally placed braces form triangles and diamonds which make a much stronger frame than horizontal struts. The cross braces span four feet (1.2 metres) and provide an ideal climbing frame for the roses. A single iron arch, or one that is not sufficiently wide, will bunch the rose growths too close together.

Originally the ironwork would have been made mostly from wrought iron which is more resistant to corrosion than the mild steel we use today. Wrought iron is now scarce and made in a limited range of sizes so we used mild steel at Warwick, but high quality hot-dipped galvanising was given to all the pieces to protect them from corrosion. The whole structure was also given a treatment to allow it to be painted straightaway because otherwise the slippery nature of the galvanising needs to weather for a season before it readily allows the paint to take a good hold.

The base plates of the feet of the arches were taken to firm subsoil and the returning soil well consolidated. Generally this is preferable to placing the feet in concrete as this can hinder drainage from the ironwork and restricts the space for planting climbers.

The tunnel arbour has been planted throughout with the rambler rose 'Albéric Barbier'. This has fully double creamy-white flowers with a good fragrance produced throughout June with some repeat flowering thereafter.

The paths throughout the garden are of stabilised gravel (clean washed gravel applied to bitumen over a tarmac base) laid to a camber and, in the tunnel arbour, given a metal strip edging. Warwick Castle and its grounds are open to the public every day of the year except Christmas Day, so a hardwearing path surface is essential.

Right. The rambler 'Adélaide d'Orléans' was chosen for the corner arbours because its flowers cascade gracefully downwards rather than facing up to the sky. The seat is a traditional fern pattern design, cast in iron and with a slatted timber seat.

Below. An individual arch with the rambler rose 'Debutante' and to the right of it the beginning of the tunnel arbour with the rambler rose 'Albéric Barbier'.

TUNNEL ARBOUR & ARCHES, VICTORIAN ROSE GARDEN, WARWICK CASTLE

The design of the layout is as a parterre garden.
The original approach from the castle was through a long tunnel arbour.
Ironwork has also been used to create an arbour & entrance arches, tripods, etc.
Outline Specification: frame members 1" × ½" [25 × 12 mm]
diagonal braces ¾" × ¼" [18 × 6mm.], welded together at crossings.
All mild steel, hot dipped galvanised & painted black, with
some gilding to cast iron finials on posts supporting the swept rails

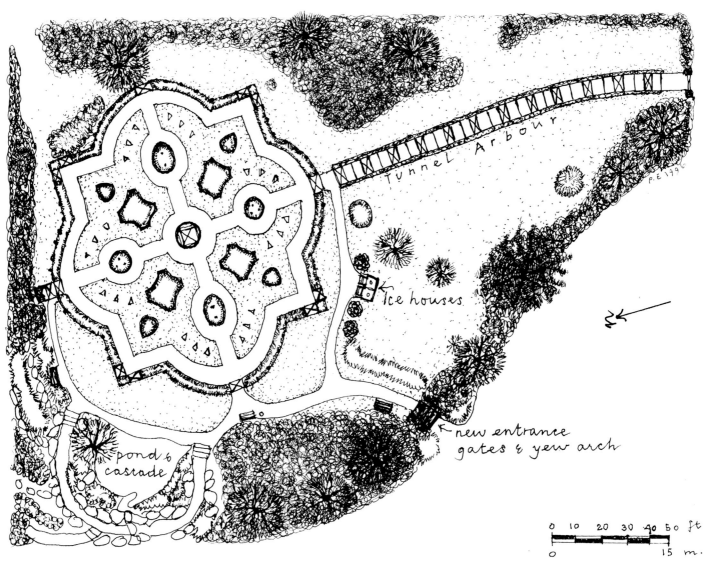

Tunnel Arbour

Ice houses

new entrance
gates & yew arch

pond &
cascade

| 0 | 10 | 20 | 30 | 40 | 50 | ft |

0   15 m.

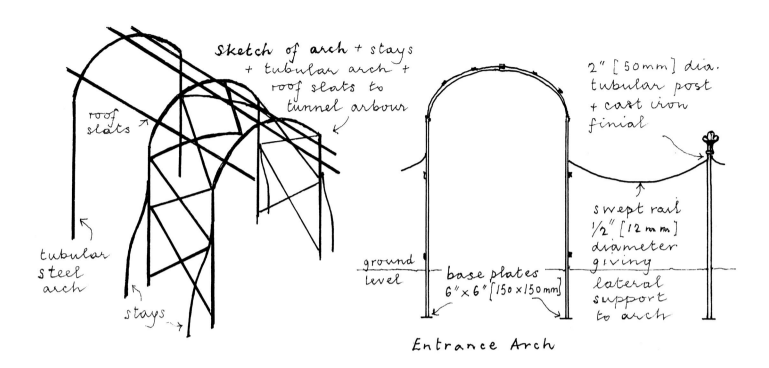

Sketch of **arch** + stays + tubular arch + roof slats to tunnel arbour

roof slats

tubular steel arch

stays

2" [50mm] dia. tubular post + cast iron finial

ground level

base plates 6" × 6" [150 × 150mm]

swept rail ½" [12mm] diameter giving lateral support to arch

Entrance Arch

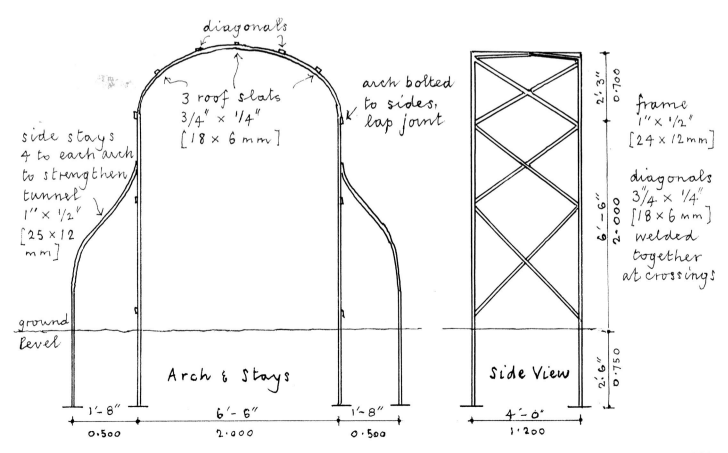

diagonals

3 roof slats 3/4" × 1/4" [18 × 6 mm]

arch bolted to sides, lap joint

side stays 4 to each arch to strengthen tunnel 1" × ½" [25 × 12 mm]

ground level

Arch & Stays

1'-8"
0.500

6'-6"
2.000

1'-8"
0.500

frame 1" × ½" [24 × 12mm]

diagonals 3/4" × 1/4" [18 × 6 mm] welded together at crossings

Side View

4'-0"
1.200

2'.3"
0.700

6'-6"
2.000

2'.6"
0.750

Lime Tunnel Arbour

Left. **The cross bracing counteracts the tensioning of the stainless steel cabling.**

The main trunks of the existing limes were cut back to encourage new lateral growths to ensure a good coverage of the tunnel.

Bluebells and forget-me-nots grow happily in the shade at the base of the lime trunks.

For many gardeners their first visit to Hidcote remains their most memorable and inspiring experience. It was the first garden to be taken over by the National Trust and the Trust is now in the process of renewing some parts of the garden.

It seems that no proper support was ever given to the tunnel of foliage that the trained and clipped lime trees provided. Over the years it had become somewhat shapeless and difficult to maintain. I was asked to design a metal support system that would be of minimal visual intrusion, strong and needing little maintenance. When I measured the tunnel I found that it tapered by about three feet (90 centimetres) over its total length of some fifty-three feet (16.15 metres) and was broadest at its entrance. In other words it had a false perspective and gave the appearance of being longer than it really was. This visual trick dates from the Renaissance and is often written about but rarely seen on the ground. It only works if the spectator arrives at the designated entrance and not the other way round. At Hidcote it works perfectly as the designed entrance is from a main terrace walk and the far end is blocked by a retaining wall with the exit a narrow opening to one side. I found this very intriguing and was tempted into measuring the nearby Long Walk of clipped hornbeam. Here again I found that the same visual device had been employed over its length from the stream to the far gateway. 'No wonder our mowing strips always overlapped at that end!' exclaimed one of the gardeners. The more one studies the garden at Hidcote, the more one comes to realise that Major Lawrence Johnston, its creator, was a most perceptive garden maker in every way.

The designed structure for the supports for the tunnel consists of stainless steel arches linked together by stainless steel cables tensioned to form the roof and sides. The pairs of arches at each end are braced to counter the overall tensioning. The shape of the arches reflects the general form of the growth of the existing limes, which was roughly in a parabolic arch. This is an unusual arch for a garden structure, but it has the merit of being structurally strong as the sloping sides reduce the need for buttressing. The arches had to be sited where gaps could be found in the closely grown rows of limes.

PARABOLIC ARCHES for LIME TUNNEL, HIDCOTE MANOR GARDEN

Note: The tunnel has "false perspective" with diminishing width of arches, but with constant height

Outline Specification : 6 no. arches in stainless steel tubes, 1½" [40 mm] dia. 6 no. stainless steel cables, ¼" [5mm] dia. + tensioners at end arches. Cross braces to both sides of end arches in stainless steel, 2"×¼" [50×5 mm] bolted to arches, curved to the arches & secured at crossings. Arches & braces painted black: base plates, 6"×6" [150×150 mm]

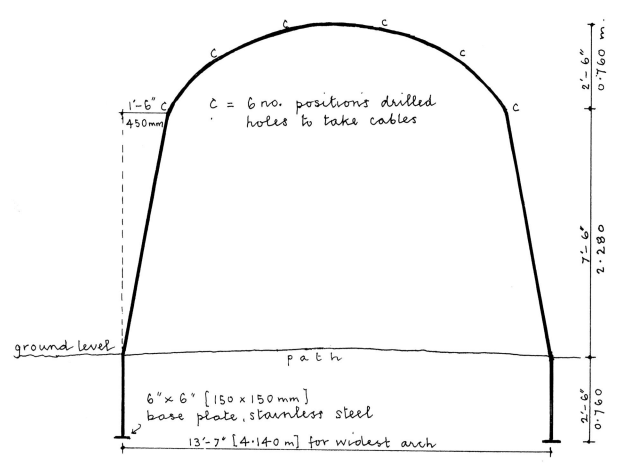

C = 6 no. positions drilled holes to take cables

1'-6" C
450mm

2'-6" 0·760 m

7'-6' 2·280

ground level

path

6"×6" [150×150 mm] base plate, stainless steel

2'-6' 0·760

13'-7" [4·140 m] for widest arch

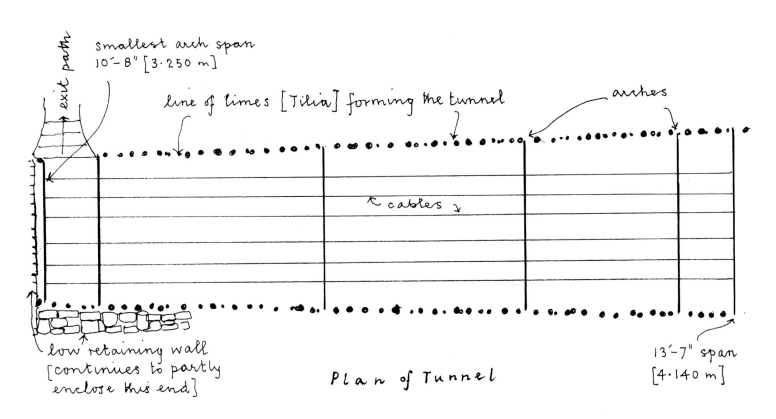

smallest arch span
10'-8" [3·250 m]

exit path

line of limes [Tilia] forming the tunnel

arches

← cables →

low retaining wall
[continues to partly
enclose this end]

Plan of Tunnel

13'-7" span
[4·140 m]

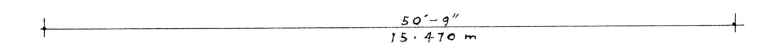

50'-9"
15·470 m

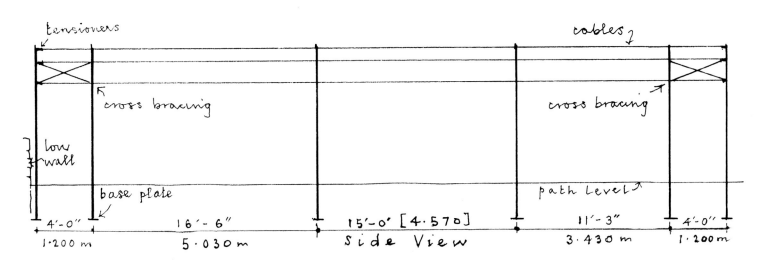

tensioners

cables →

cross bracing

cross bracing

low
wall

base plate

path level

4'-0"

16'-6"

15'-0' [4·570]

11'-3"

4'-0"

1·200 m

5·030 m

Side View

3·430 m

1·200 m

155

Rustic Yew Arch and Topiary Arch

Left. The rustic yew arch in its setting on a main vista in the Old Garden.

Arch in clipped yew between the White Garden and the Maple Garden at Hidcote.

There was a decaying timber arch supporting some climbers in the Old Garden next to the house at Hidcote and I was asked to prepare an appropriate design for something to take its place. The existing structure was itself of little merit but had replaced an earlier arch. The question was what the original structure in Lawrence Johnston's garden had been like, so we asked Graham Stuart Thomas, who had been Gardens Consultant to the National Trust, what he remembered about the arch. He described it as having been in rustic work with the outline of a pediment at each end.

Much recent rustic work has been made from closely trimmed larch but once this has lost its bark it does not have much character left. Descriptions of elaborate rustic work in Victorian gardens suggested that yew, with its long-lasting qualities and the most attractive colouring of our native timbers, should be used. The problem was collecting enough stout pieces, particularly for the posts. As it happened a mature beech had recently crashed into a large yew tree at Stanway and Lord Neidpath kindly allowed myself and the carpenter to select suitable branches. We found a few more pieces on the Hidcote estate itself and were able to construct the yew arch on site. The side branches were not cut off flush but were left with short snags to give a more twiggy look. The arch below shows what can be done with living yew.

RUSTIC YEW ARCH for the OLD GARDEN, HIDCOTE MANOR GARDEN

Constructed in yew branches plus bark, with side shoots not cut off flush, but left twiggy

Joints to be drilled to take long wood screws, counter-sunk & wax plugged. Posts 4" [100mm] approx. diameter.

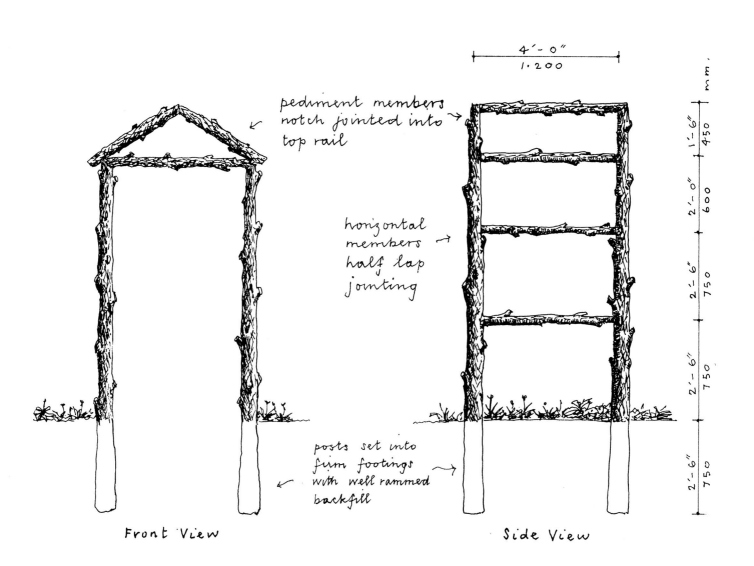

pediment members notch jointed into top rail

horizontal members half lap jointing

posts set into firm footings with well rammed backfill

4'-0"
1·200

1'-6"   450
2'-0"   600
2'-6"   750
2'-6"   750
2'-6"   750
mm.

Front View

Side View

DESIGN for a YEW ARCHWAY

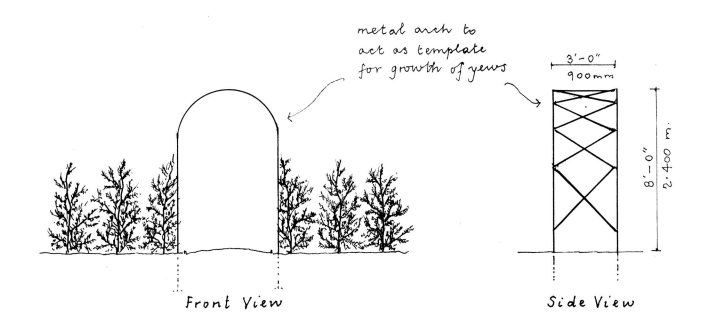

metal arch to
act as template
for growth of yews

3'-0"
900mm

8'-0"
2.400 m

Front View

Side View

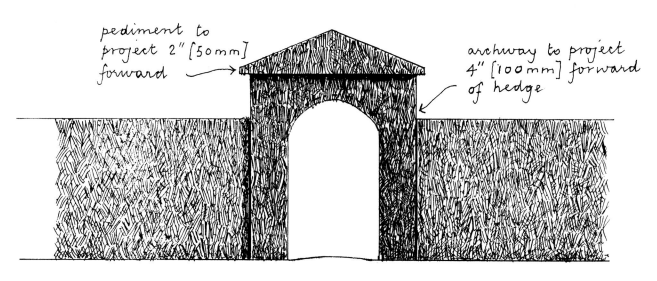

pediment to
project 2" [50mm]
forward

archway to project
4" [100mm] forward
of hedge

Fully Grown Archway

DRAWINGS SHOWING DETAILS OF PERGOLA CONSTRUCTION

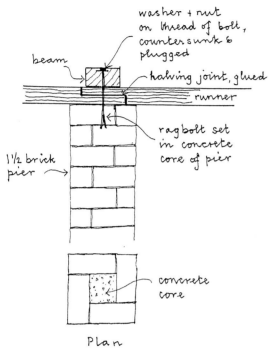

washer + nut on thread of bolt, countersunk & plugged

beam

halving joint, glued

runner

1½ brick pier

ragbolt set in concrete core of pier

concrete core

Plan

Top of brick pier of Pergola

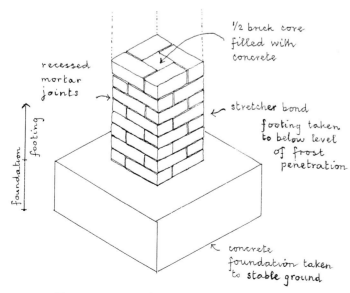

½ brick core filled with concrete

recessed mortar joints

stretcher bond

footing taken to below level of frost penetration

foundation footing

concrete foundation taken to stable ground

1½ Brick Pier for a Pergola

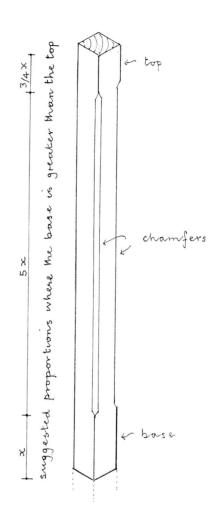

top

¾ x

5 x

suggested proportions where the base is greater than the top

chamfers

base

x

Stop Chamfers to Timber Posts of Pergola

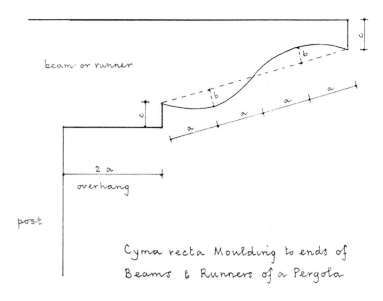

coach screw & washer
countersunk & plugged

halving
joint, glued

beam

runner

runner notched
into post

post

Top of timber Pergola

beam or runner

2 a
overhang

post

Cyma recta Moulding to ends of
Beams & Runners of a Pergola

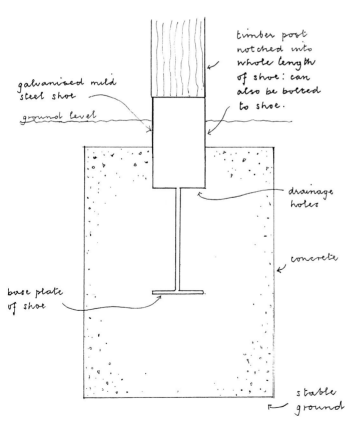

timber post
notched into
whole length
of shoe: can
also be bolted
to shoe.

galvanised mild
steel shoe

ground level

drainage
holes

concrete

base plate
of shoe

stable
ground

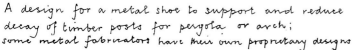

A design for a metal shoe to support and reduce
decay of timber posts for pergola or arch;
some metal fabricators have their own proprietary designs

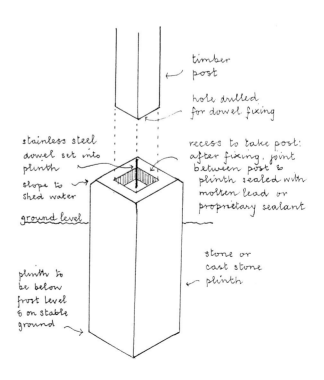

timber
post

hole drilled
for dowel fixing

stainless steel
dowel set into
plinth

slope to
shed water

ground level

recess to take post:
after fixing, joint
between post &
plinth sealed with
molten lead or
proprietary sealant

stone or
cast stone
plinth

plinth to
be below
frost level
& on stable
ground

Plinth Support for Timber Pergola Post

SHAPES FOR ARCHES

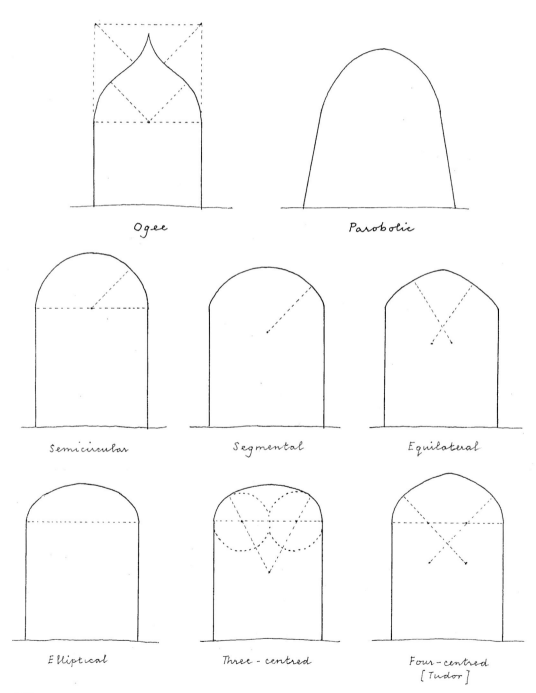

Ogee

Parobolic

Semicircular

Segmental

Equilateral

Elliptical

Three - centred

Four - centred
[Tudor]

Gardens to Visit

It would be impractical to list every garden with a good pergola. The following is a list of those gardens in England and Wales featured in this book and open to the public. It is recommended that opening times are checked with the gardens or institutions concerned.

Ashridge
Governors of Ashridge
Berkhamsted, Hertfordshire HP4 1NS.
Tel. 01442 843491

Barrington Court
The National Trust
Barrington, nr Ilminster,
Somerset TA19 0NQ. Tel. 01460 241938

Bodnant Garden
The National Trust
Tal-y-Cafn, Colwyn Bay, Conwy,
Wales Ll28 5RE. Tel 01492 650460

Chartwell
The National Trust
Westerham, Kent TN16 1PS.
Tel.01732 866368

The Dower House Gardens
Katherine Swift
Morville Hall, nr Bridgnorth,
Shropshire WV16 5NB.
Tel. 01746 714407

Easton Lodge
Brian Creasey
Great Dunmow,
Essex CM6 2BB. Tel. 01371 876979

Fishbourne Roman Palace
Sussex Archaeological Society
Salthill Road, Fishbourne, Chichester,
Sussex PO19 3QR. Tel. 01243 785859

The Gardens of the Rose
Royal National Rose Society
Chiswell Green, St Albans,
Hertfordshire AL2 3NR.
Tel. 01727 850461

Gravetye Manor
Privately owned hotel
nr East Grinstead RH19 4LJ.
Tel.01342 810567

Great Fosters
Privately owned hotel
Stroude Road, Egham, Surrey.
Tel. 01784 433822

Greys Court
The National Trust
Rotherfield Greys, Henley-on-Thames,
Oxfordshire RG9 4PG.
Tel. 01491 628529

Ham House
The National Trust
Ham, Richmond, London TW10 7RS.
Tel. 020 8940 1950

Hampton Court Palace
Hitoric Royal Palaces
East Molesey, Surrey KT8 9AU.
Tel. 020 8781 9500

Heale House Garden
Mr and Mrs Guy Rasch
Middle Woodford, Salisbury,
Wiltshire SP4 6NT. Tel. 01722 782504

Helmingham Hall Gardens
Lord and Lady Tollemache
Helmingham Hall, Stowmarket,
Suffolk IP14 6EF. Tel. 01473 890363

Hestercombe House Gardens
Somerset County Council
Hestercombe, Cheddon Fitzpaine,
Taunton, Somerset TA2 8LG.
Tel. 01823 413923

Hidcote Manor Garden
The National Trust
Hidcote Bartrim, nr Chipping
Campden, Gloucestershire GL55 6LR.
Tel. 01684 855370

Kiftsgate Court
Mr and Mrs J.G.Chambers
Chipping Campden, Gloucestershire
GL55 6LW. Tel. 01386 438777

The Manor House Garden
Ros Wallinger
Upton Grey, Basingstoke, Hampshire.
Tel. 01256 862827
(by appointment only)

Moseley Old Hall
The National Trust
Moseley Old Hall Lane, Fordhouses,
Wolverhampton, Staffordshire
WV10 7HY. Tel. 01902 782808

Mottisfont Abbey Garden
The National Trust
Mottisfont, nr Romsey,
Hampshire SO51 0LP.
Tel. 01794 340757

Museum of Garden History
The Tradescant Trust
Lambeth Palace Road, London SE1 7LB.
Tel. 020 7401 8865

Nymans Garden
The National Trust
Handcross, nr Haywards Heath, West
Sussex RH17 6EB. Tel. 01444 400321

Otley Hall
Nicholas and Ann Hagger
Otley, nr Ipswich, Suffolk IP6 9PA.
Tel. 01473 890264

Painswick Rococo Gardens
Painswick Rococo Garden Trust
The Stables, Painswick House,
Painswick, Gloucestershire GL6 6TH.
Tel. 01452 813204

Polesden Lacey
The National Trust
Great Bookham, nr Dorking, Surrey
RH5 6BD. Tel. 01372 452048

Queen Eleanor's Garden
Hampshire County Council
Great Hall, The Castle, Winchester,
Hampshire Tel. 01962 840476

The Hill
Corporation of London
Inverforth Close, off North End Way,
Hampstead, London NW11.
Tel. 020 8455 5183

Tretower Court
Cadw: Welsh Historic Monuments
Crickhowell, Powys NP8 2RF.
Tel. 01874 730279

Waddesdon Manor
The National Trust
Waddesdon, nr Aylesbury,
Buckinghamshire HP18 0JH.
Tel. 01296 653212

Warwick Castle
Tussauds Group Ltd
Warwick, Warwickshire CV34 4QU.
Tel. 01926 406600

West Dean Gardens
The Edward James Foundation
West Dean, Chichester, West Sussex
PO18 0QZ. Tel. 01243 818210

Books, Acknowledgements and Illustration Credits

Books to read

Contemporary sources are noted in the relevant chapters of the book. The following list aims to identify the most useful general books for each period.

Roman
Linda Farrar, *Ancient Roman Gardens* (Sutton, 1998)
W.F.Jashemski, *The Gardens of Pompeii…* (2 vols, New Rochelle, 1979)

Medieval
John Harvey, *Mediaeval Gardens* (Batsford, 1981)
Sylvia Landsberg, *The Medieval Garden* (British Museum, 1995)

Renaissance and Baroque
David Jacques and Arend Jan van der Horst *The Gardens of William and Mary* (Christopher Helm, 1988)
Roy Strong, *The Renaissance Garden in England* (Thames and Hudson 1979)
Kenneth Woodbridge, *Princely Gardens* (Thames and Hudson, 1986)

Victorian and Arts and Crafts
Brent Elliott, *Victorian Gardens* (Batsford, 1986)
David Ottewill, *The Edwardian Garden* (Yale, 1989)

Modern
Alan Blanc, *Landscape Construction and Detailing* (Batsford, 1996)
Jane Brown, *The English Garden in the Twentieth Century* (Garden Art Press, 1999)

Illustration credits

All photographs are by Jessica Smith and all drawings by Paul Edwards unless noted below. Where the sources of other illustrations have not been given in the text they are as listed here. Requests for permission to reproduce illustrations from this book should be addressed firstly to the publisher.

page 8 top and bottom © The British Museum
page 9 J.Gardiner Wilkinson, *The Ancient Egyptians* (London, 1853)
page 13 Staatliche Museen zu Berlin – Preussischer Kulturbesitz Antikensammlung. Photograph Christa Begall
page 14 top *Pompeii: Its History, Buildings and Antiquities*, ed. T.H.Dyer (2nd ed., London, 1868)
page 14 bottom W.F.Jashemski, *The Gardens of Pompeii…* (2, 1993)
page 15 (1) Museo Nazionale Archeologico, Naples. Inv. 9964
page 15 (2 and 4) Taken from Daremberg and Saglio, *Dictionnaire des Antiquités, Grecques et Romaines* (Paris, 1900)
page 15 (3) Redrawn by Linda Farrar from Daremberg as above.
page 16 Antonio Ferrua, *The Unknown Catacomb* (New Lanark, 1991)
page 17 The Metropolitan Museum of Art, Rogers Fund, 1903 (03.14.13) Photograph © 1986 The Metropolitan Museum of Art
page 18 Linda Farrar
page 20 and 30 bottom right Foto Baumgartner, Graz, Austria © Stift Melk
page 21 Bodleian Library, University of Oxford. MS Douce 31, fol.232b recto
page 22 Detail from re-drawing of Wibert's plan by R.Willis. Kent Archaeological Society
page 23 Scala/Oratorio di S.Giovanni Battista, Urbino
page 24 Bibliothèque nationale de France
page 25 Scala/Museo di Castelvecchio, Verona
page 26 bottom Drawing by Sylvia Landsberg
pages 28 and 29 Kerstin Holmberg
page 30 top and bottom left Drawings by Sylvia Landsberg
page 34 © Tate, London 2001
page 39 Scala/Museo di Firenze com'era, Florence
page 41 The Royal Collection © 2001, Her Majesty Queen Elizabeth II

page 53 National Trust Photographic Library
page 60 Country Life Picture Library
page 61 © National Monuments Record
page 63 Christopher Wood Gallery
page 68 top Frances Wells
page 68 bottom Jan Woudstra
page 69 Andrew Clayden
page 72 top Andrew Clayden
page 79 bottom Jan Woudstra
page 73 Andrew Clayden
page 76 top and centre left © Crown copyright – National Monuments Record
page 76 centre right Country Life Picture Library
page 76 bottom left The Edward James Foundation
page 76 bottom right Country Life Picture Library
page 80 Country Life Picture Library
page 81 © Crown copyright – National Monuments Record
page 88 Country Life Picture Library
page 91 and 92 Country Life Picture Library
page 98 right and 99 bottom The Edward James Foundation
page 104 top © Pan-Aero Pictures, Kingston on Thames (photograph National Monuments Record)
page 104 bottom Country Life Picture Library
page 145 Paul Edwards

Acknowledgements

The authors and publisher would like to thank the following for their generous help and advice in the preparation of this book:

Mavis Batey, Jim Buckland, Susan Campbell, John, Richard, Edmund and Ben Crawley, Roger Dalladay, Mark Davis, Lord Dickinson, Russell Dixon, Diana Ford, Teresa Francis, Dagmar Glausnitzer, Keith Goodway, Geoff Green, Peter Hayden, Kerstin Holmberg, Sally Hocking, Caroline Holmes, Margaret Howatson, John Humphries, Stanley Ireland, Anne Jennings, Harriet Jordan, Sharon-Michi Kusunoki, Brenda Lewis, J-P Marix Evans, Laurence Pattacini, Martin Puddle, Jonathan Shaw, Sandra Schwartz, Cyril Taylor, Kristina Taylor, David Usher, Sarah Wain, Ros Wallinger, Elisabeth Whittle, Kim Wilkie, Christopher Wood and William Ziemba.

Index

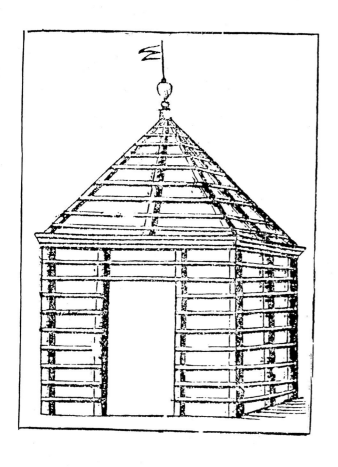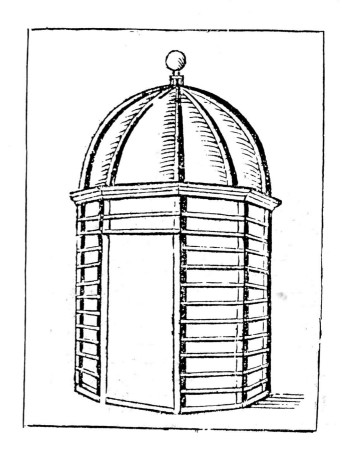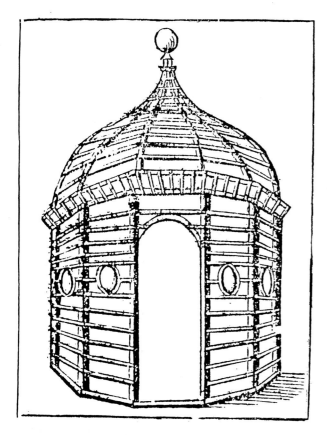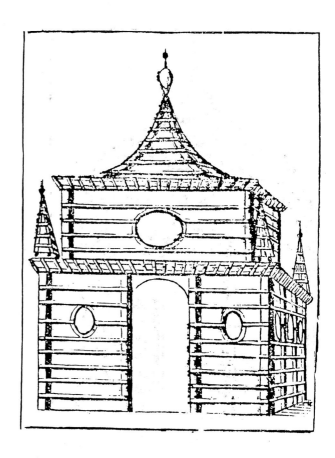